Sinbadala

A pantomime

Richard Lloyd

Samuel French — London
www.samuelfrench-london.co.uk

© 2010 by Richard Lloyd

Rights of Performance by Amateurs are controlled by Samuel French Ltd, 52 Fitzroy Street, London W1T 5JR, and they, or their authorized agents, issue licences to amateurs on payment of a fee. **It is an infringement of the Copyright to give any performance or public reading of the play before the fee has been paid and the licence issued.**

The Royalty Fee indicated below is subject to contract and subject to variation at the sole discretion of Samuel French Ltd.

Basic fee for each and every
    performance by amateurs   Code K
    in the British Isles

The publication of this play does not imply that it is necessarily available for performance by amateurs or professionals, either in the British Isles or Overseas. Amateurs and professionals considering a production are strongly advised in their own interests to apply to the appropriate agents for written consent before starting rehearsals or booking a theatre or hall.

The right of Richard Lloyd to be identified as author of this work has been asserted by him in accordance with Section 77 of the Copyright, Designs and Patents Act 1988

ISBN 978 0 573 16447 7

Please see page v for further copyright information

SINBADALADDIN!

First presented by Theatre Workshop Coulsdon on Saturday 13th December 2008, with the following cast:

Widow Twankee	John East
Wishee-Washee	Neil Grew
Sinbad	Emma Griffin
Hoo-Poo	Luke Argles
Hee-Pong	Mike Brown
The Grand Vizier	Bruce Montgomery
Abanazar	Chris Blakeney
The Slave of the Ring	Steve North
Aladdin	Kimberley Argles
Princess Jasmine	Dee Ajiba
No-Lo-Fat	Rosie Martin
Ming the Mirthless	Chris Argles
Chip-Chop-Ow	Andy Wiggins
Pee-Long	Pip Martin
Mrs Cheng	Tanya Allison
Nip-Tuk	Lisa Lloyd
Kung Po Prawn	Fiona Harrison
Wong-Ki-I	John Bird
Wong-Wei	Tim Young
The Slave of the Lamp	Penny Payne
Herald of the Imperial Court	Tania Gauci
Noo-Noo, a pantomime panda	Robyn Doran
Imperial Messengers	Morgan Lloyd
	James North
Yangtze Pirates	Becca Blanchard
	Eloise Brown
	Dawn Lock
	Hannah Montgomery
	Jonathan North
	Lindsey Riches

COPYRIGHT INFORMATION

(See also page ii)

This play is fully protected under the Copyright Laws of the British Commonwealth of Nations, the United States of America and all countries of the Berne and Universal Copyright Conventions.

All rights including Stage, Motion Picture, Radio, Television, Public Reading, and Translation into Foreign Languages, are strictly reserved.

No part of this publication may lawfully be reproduced in ANY form or by any means — photocopying, typescript, recording (including video-recording), manuscript, electronic, mechanical, or otherwise—or be transmitted or stored in a retrieval system, without prior permission.

Licences for amateur performances are issued subject to the understanding that it shall be made clear in all advertising matter that the audience will witness an amateur performance; that the names of the authors of the plays shall be included on all programmes; and that the integrity of the authors' work will be preserved.

The Royalty Fee is subject to contract and subject to variation at the sole discretion of Samuel French Ltd.

In Theatres or Halls seating Four Hundred or more the fee will be subject to negotiation.

In Territories Overseas the fee quoted above may not apply. A fee will be quoted on application to our local authorized agent, or if there is no such agent, on application to Samuel French Ltd, London.

VIDEO-RECORDING OF AMATEUR PRODUCTIONS

Please note that the copyright laws governing video-recording are extremely complex and that it should not be assumed that any play may be video-recorded for whatever purpose without first obtaining the permission of the appropriate agents. The fact that a play is published by Samuel French Ltd does not indicate that video rights are available or that Samuel French Ltd controls such rights.

CHARACTERS

Widow Twankee, proprietress of the Happy Tub Chinese Laundry — M
Aladdin, her good-for-nothing son (later, Prince Wai-No-Dong) — F
Sinbad the Sailor, an itinerant principal boy — F
Wishee-Washee, slopper-out of the Happy Tub — M
Abanazar, a magician — M
Hoo-Poo, a Chinese policeman — M
Hee-Pong, ditto — M
Dim Sum, a Pekingese police dog puppet (*in a basket on the front of a bicycle...*)
Ming the Mirthless, Sultan of Ching-Chong, Ping-Pong and Ooooagadoogoo — M
No-Lo-Fat, the Sultana — F
Princess Jasmine, fragrant and delectable — F
Pee-Long, her hand maiden — F
The Grand Vizier — M
Chip-Chop-Ow, the inscrutable executioner — M
The Slave of the Ring — M
The Slave of the Lamp — F
Mrs Cheng, terrifying piratical personage — F
Nip-Tuk — F
Kung Po Prawn — F
Wong-Ki-I — M
Wong-Wei — M
⎱ Mrs Cheng's cut-throat crew of Yangtze River pirate scum ⎰
Noo-Noo, a pantomime panda — F
Herald of the Imperial Court — M/F
Coolies, Pirates, and Citizens of Old Peking
Pianist

SYNOPSIS OF SCENES

ACT I
Scene 1 *A Street in Old Peking*
Scene 2 *The Tent of Abanazar*
Scene 3 *The Happy Tub Chinese Laundry*
Scene 4 *Tabs*
Scene 5 *A clearing*
Scene 6 *The Happy Tub Chinese Laundry*
Scene 7 *A Street in Old Peking (Tabs)*
Scene 8 *Outside the Cave of a Thousand Rubies (Tabs)*
Scene 9 *Inside the Cave of a Thousand Rubies*

ACT II
Scene 1 *Ming the Mirthless' Throneroom*
Scene 2 *A clearing*
Scene 3 *The Happy Tub Chinese Laundry*
Scene 4 *A Street Scene*
Scene 5 *Another Street Scene*
Scene 6 *Aladdin's Palace*
Scene 7 *Ming the Mirthless' Throneroom*

COPYRIGHT MUSIC

The notice printed below on behalf of the Performing Right Society should be carefully read if any copyright music is used in this play.

The permission of the owner of the performing rights in copyright music must be obtained before any public performance may be given, whether in conjunction with a play or sketch or otherwise, and this permission is just as necessary for amateur performances as for professional. The majority of copyright musical works (other than oratorios, musical plays and similar dramatico-musical works) are controlled in the British Commonwealth by the PERFORMING RIGHT SOCIETY LTD, 29-33 Berners Street, London W1P 4AA.

The Society's practice is to issue licences authorizing the use of its repertoire to the proprietors of premises at which music is publicly performed, or, alternatively, to the organizers of musical entertainments, but the Society does not require payment of fees by performers as such. Producers or promoters of plays, sketches, etc., at which music is to be performed, during or after the play or sketch, should ascertain whether the premises at which their performances are to be given are covered by a licence issued by the Society, and if they are not, should make application to the Society for particulars as to the fee payable.

A separate and additional licence from PHONOGRAPHIC PERFORMANCES LTD, 1 Upper James Street, London W1R 3HG, is needed whenever commercial recordings are used.

MUSICAL NUMBERS

ACT I

Overture	Company
Song 1	Wishee-Washee and Widow Twankee
Song 2	Aladdin and Princess Jasmine
Song 3	Hoo-Poo and Hee-Pong
Song 4	Aladdin
Song 5	Pirates
Song 6	Abanazar

ACT II

Song 7	Mrs Cheng and Two Pirate Dancers
Song 8	Widow Twankee/Audience
Song 9	Aladdin, Princess Jasmine, The Slave of The Lamp and The Slave of The Ring
Song 10	Aladdin and Princess Jasmine, Sinbad and Pee-Long, Widow Twankee and the Grand Vizier, Ming the Mirthless and No-Lo-Fat, and Wishee-Washee
Song 11	Company

AUTHOR'S NOTE

This pantomime is essentially Aladdin with a dash of Sinbad, plus a few other surprise oriental ingredients thrown in. Being a souped-up version of Aladdin, there are two larger-than life genies, which means lots of magical bangs and flashes. If your facilities (or production budget) won't run to this level of pyrotechnic extravagance, there is of course the good old blackout and cymbal clash combo.

Take a look at any script of Aladdin, and you'll see lots of comic pidgin 'Chinese' dialogue – it's always been part of the essential fun of this pantomime. In this script, only the three obviously comic characters (Wishee-Washee and the two Chinese policemen) speak in pastiche oriental, whilst the Yangtse pirates are a kind of cross between Chinese, piratical, and indeterminably non-English. This is easily adjusted if you aren't comfortable with this aspect of the tradition. Similarly, a number of corny 'Chinese' jokes - many of which you've probably heard before – have been included in the broker's men routine in Act Two, Scene Three. Again, any of these can be omitted or substituted at the discretion of the producing society.

Including eleven musical numbers and two dance routines, the running time of the original production was one hour and ten minutes in each half. If a shorter running time is required, I suggest songs four and seven are omitted.

Richard Lloyd

For Kimberley
Brilliant principal boy

Other pantomimes by Richard Lloyd:

Arabian Knights - The Panto!
The Christmas Cavalier
Smut's Saga, or, Santa and the Vikings
The Three Musketeers - le Panteau!
Treasure Island - the Panto

ACT I

Scene 1

Overture, leading into... A street in Old Peking. An overhead sign reads "Old Peking" in suitably oriental lettering. There are pagodas to either side, and strings of colourful Chinese lanterns suspended between them. Curtains *open on to a huge pastiche Mikado-style opening*

The entire cast enter and bustle around in a vibrant oriental street scene, bowing to each other and so on. After a few moments they form up into a stagey tableau to sing the big opening number... The music swells to a mighty build-up. In perfect harmony the assembled company lustily sing...

Company "Welcome to Old Peking..."

They take a deep breath as if to continue – then think better of it. The tableau breaks up and all scamper off in different directions while the music continues, leaving only Widow Twankee on stage. She tries in vain to stop one or two of the departing company, and ends up shouting after them

Widow Twankee 'Ere! Where are you all going? Is that it? Oi! Come back! It's supposed to be the spectacular opening number...

The music fizzles out

(*To audience*) Oh well, there you go. That's your lot. "Welcome to Old Peking". And I mean it — you're welcome to Old Peking. I mean, honestly — what a dump. Have you ever seen such pathetic scenery? ...Still, never mind, you're here now, that's the main thing... Ooooh, I do apologize — I haven't introduced myself. Widow Twankee, at your service. Queen bee of the wash-tub business. Proprietor and head scrubber of the world famous Happy Tub Chinese Laundry. If there's a bigger scrubber on the face of the planet, I'd like to meet her... (*Picking on a member of the audience*) Yes? Oh I'm sorry... I thought that man in the third row put his hand up. Yes, you sir. Is that your wife? Ah, I see... Anyway... I just popped out from the laundry to see if I could find Aladdin. Do you know Aladdin? He's my son you know... Oh, he's a charming rogue. Good-looking, quick-witted — and lazy as a fat Mandarin after a seventeen course banquet. Honestly — I love him dearly — but if you've ever met a more workshy loafer, I'll boil me bum in me own tub. Takes after his father, of course. Oh, he was an idle good-for-nothing. He was so idle, that one day he went to sleep and never woke up again. 'E just — stopped. So... we don't want that to happen to Aladdin, do we?

Audience participation

Bicycle bell off

Oh look out. Here we go...

Wishee-Washee enters furiously pedalling a tricycle

Wishee-Washee Widow Twankee, Widow Twankee!
Widow Twankee Wishee-Washee, Wishee-Washee!
Wishee-Washee What?
Widow Twankee Nothing.
Wishee-Washee Oh.
Widow Twankee Well?
Wishee-Washee Well what?
Widow Twankee Oh for Pete's sake... (*To the audience*) This, ladies and gentlemen, boys and girls, is Wishee-Washee, chief slopper-out at the Happy Tub Chinese laundry. He's my helper... 'cept he's no help whatsoever.
Wishee-Washee Widow Twankee? Where Aladdin go?
Widow Twankee I don't know, do I? I sent you out to look for him.
Wishee-Washee (*remembering*) Oh yeah...
Widow Twankee So did you find him?
Wishee-Washee (*crestfallen*) Oh no.
Widow Twankee (*to audience*) See what I mean? Completely useless. I don't know where that boy's got to. Always makes himself scarce when there's work to be done at the laundry. 'Ere, will you lot do me a favour and keep an eye out for him?

Audience participation

Will you?... Oh that is kind. Tell you what, if you see him, just give me a shout will you? Shout "Oi Twankee!" and I'll be there like a rat up a drainpipe. Can you do that? Let's have a practice shall we? After three – one, two, three...

Act I, Scene 1

Audience participation

Oh blimey... Come on — you can do better than that. Let's try again... One, two, three...

Audience participation

Much better! Right. See you later then... Oooh. Hang on a mo — I've just remembered: You don't even know what Aladdin looks like, do you? So I'll tell you. He's the principal boy he is. You'll recognize him straightaway, 'cos he's tall, slim and foxy as hell. He's wearing a short tunic, long boots, and 'e slaps his thigh a lot. Like this... (*She slaps her thigh*)

Wishee-Washee (*looking on with interest*) Can I do that?
Widow Twankee Course you can...
Wishee-Washee (*slapping Widow Twankee hard on the thigh and looking pleased with himself*) Thanks.
Widow Twankee (*wincing*) Pleasure.
Wishee-Washee Rubbery.
Widow Twankee I'm sorry?
Wishee-Washee Rubbery.
Widow Twankee You mean lovely?
Wishee-Washee No, I mean rubbery. Like blubbery.

Song 1 (Wishee-Washee and Widow Twankee)

After the song Widow Twankee launches herself at Wishee-Washee. He ducks out of her way as she reaches out to throttle him. She chases him off L

A moment later Sinbad saunters on R. *He has a bundle wrapped in a spotted handkerchief slung from a stick over his shoulder, and he wears a raffish turban. Apart from that, he's dressed like a principal boy — short, belted tunic, waistcoat, fishnet tights, long boots. He stops, looks around, peers at the audience, and then... slaps his thigh*

The audience — not unreasonably assuming him to be Aladdin — chorus:

Audience Oi Twankee!

Widow Twankee rushes back on, followed by Wishee-Washee, who keeps a safe distance

Widow Twankee Yes?! Yes?! Blimey, that was quick — have you found him? Have you found Aladdin?

Audience participation

You have? Where is he then?

Audience participation (there!)

That's not Aladdin.

Audience participation

Oh no it's not. (*To Sinbad*) Who are you?
Sinbad I am Sinbad.
Widow Twankee What, the sailor?

Sinbad nods

You're lost.
Sinbad Ha! I'm the most famous navigator in the world. How can I be lost?
Widow Twankee 'Cos you're in the wrong panto, mate.
Sinbad I needed a change of scene.
Widow Twankee (*glancing disparagingly at the scenery*) Well you'll be lucky to get one of those round here... What do you do then?
Sinbad I'm a principal boy.
Widow Twankee Oh no you're not, because my Aladdin, he's principal boy — see.
Sinbad Well there's room enough for two, isn't there?
Widow Twankee No.
Sinbad Why not?
Widow Twankee 'Cos we're in Old Peking — the city of all cities. It's Aladdin, isn't it! Only the most famous flippin' story in "The Arabian Nights".
Sinbad Well I'm in "The Arabian Nights" too.
Widow Twankee Yeah — on the other side of the ruddy continent. Not in the mysterious Orient. Besides, we can't have two principal boys. That'd be all wrong.
Sinbad Would you like to hear about my seven incredible voyages?
Wishee-Washee Yeah!
Widow Twankee No.
Sinbad Oh.

Act I, Scene 1

Widow Twankee But we would like to know what you're doing in the wrong panto...
Sinbad Let's just say I need to keep a low profile for a while.
Widow Twankee Got up someone's hooter did you?
Sinbad You could say that...
Widow Twankee Who?
Sinbad Mrs Cheng.
Widow Twankee Mrs Cheng? Not Mrs Cheng, Queen of the Yangtze Pirates.
Sinbad Might be.
Widow Twankee Mrs Cheng, the most terrifying female pirate in the blood-spattered history of piracy.
Sinbad That's her.
Widow Twankee (*digesting this information*) Right... Go on, hoppit. Sling your hook. We don't need your sort round here. We've got quite enough to put up with, without hordes of bloodthirsty pirates swarming down on us.
Sinbad But...
Widow Twankee No buts. Push off.
Sinbad But...
Widow Twankee OFF!
Sinbad Very well...

Sinbad's shoulders slump as he traipses sadly offstage

Wishee-Washee (*to the audience*) Aaaaaaaah...
Audience Aaaaaaaaaaaaah.
Widow Twankee Oh don't waste your sympathy on him, ladies and gentlemen, boys and girls. Pantoland is full of these out-of-work layabouts... They can't just go round hijacking other people's adventures. It would upset the whole balance of the sauce.
Wishee-Washee What's the sauce?
Widow Twankee Well, you know like in Star Wars, they have "The Force"?
Wishee-Washee Yeah?
Widow Twankee Well in panto, we have the sauce.
Wishee-Washee Ah – like mystical, unseen, spirit of pantomime, yes?
Widow Twankee No. It's more like splurge foam. Here... (*Reaching offstage*) May the sauce be with you. (*She splats a custard pie in his face*)

Wishee-Washee blinks at her through a mask of foam

Anyway, speaking of out-of-work layabouts, I've got something for you.
Wishee-Washee What?
Widow Twankee This. (*Clipping him round the ear*) Now get on your flippin' bike and get back to the laundry! And if you see Aladdin, tell him he'd better make himself useful or he's going to find himself out of work, and out of a role too. Off you go...

Wishee-Washee mounts his tricycle and pedals furiously R

Hoo-Poo (*off*) Make way! Make way!
Widow Twankee Oh no — get shot of one idiot, and two more appear in his place...

Hoo-Poo, one of the Chinese policemen, enters L *on foot with a besom broom and a megaphone slung round his neck. He sweeps right up to Widow Twankee's boots, then repeats officiously*

Hoo-Poo Make way! Make way!

Widow Twankee glowers at him and refuses to budge. Hoo-Poo raises his megaphone right in her face and bellows

Make way! Make way!

Still she refuses to move. Hoo-Poo eyes her up. He knows a troublemaker when he sees one. He turns and bellows offstage through his megaphone

Hee-Pong! Blues and twos I think...

Hee-Pong enters, riding a bone-shaker bicycle with a basket mounted on the handlebars. He cycles round in a circle waving a blue flag and making siren noises

Hee-Pong Nee-naw nee-naw nee-naw!
Widow Twankee Pathetic.

Hoo-Poo starts sweeping around Widow Twankee. Hee-Pong parks his bike to one side, climbs off and adjusts his trousers

Well, well. If it isn't Hoo-Poo and Hee-Pong, Peking's answer to Starsky and Hutch (*or insert topical detective duo*). And what are you two numpties up to?
Hee-Pong The Grand Vizier, he say go make thorough sweep of route.

Act I, Scene 1

Widow Twankee Route?
Hoo-Poo Her Fragrant Delectableness, Princess Jasmine, Daughter of his Imperial Highness, Ming the Mirthless, Sultan of Ching-Chong, Ping-Pong, and Oooooagadoogoo...
Hee-Pong Is taking a dip...
Hoo-Poo At the Bath-house of Heavenly Delight.
Widow Twankee Blimey... That's what all the fuss is about? Bathtime for some spoiled little Palace chit.
Hoo-Poo Yeah! And no common coolie is allowed to set beady eyes on her most Royal and Imperial Scrumptiousness...
Hee-Pong Yeah! On pain of deaf!
Widow Twankee (*correcting him*) Death.
Hee-Pong Yeah — that right! ...So we sweeping route of all raff-riff.
Hoo-Poo So go takee-walkee, or it'll be chip-chop-ow for you.
Widow Twankee Ooooh how dare you! I'll have you know I'm not riff-raff. I'm quality I am. A high class scrubber.
Hoo-Poo Oh yeah? We soon see.
Widow Twankee How?
Hoo-Poo Hee Pong...
Widow Twankee (*aside; to audience*) Yes he does...
Hoo-Poo Deploy the sniffer dog.
Hee-Pong Deploy sniffer dog! (*Picking the basket off the front of the bike and inserting his forearm through a false bottom in the basket*) Dim Sum — walkies!

Dim Sum — a small tousled Pekingese glove puppet — looks out of his basket and yips manically

Widow Twankee (*to audience*) Oh look — shweeeeeeeeeeeeeeeet!

Dim Sum yips some more and tries to bite her finger

Hoo-Poo This Dim Sum — Peking Police Department number one sniffer dog.
Widow Twankee Shitzou?
Hee-Pong There's no need to be rude.
Hoo-Poo Actually, he's a Pekingese.
Widow Twankee (*pointing at the sign saying "Old Peking"*) Durr, well obviously...
Hoo-Poo He specially trained to sniff out coolies, peasants and similar low-grade rubbish.
Widow Twankee (*intrigued*) Really? How does he do that then?
Hoo-Poo Easy — coolies, peasants and low-grade rubbish smell like doggy-doos...

Hee-Pong Which he likes…

Dim Sum yaps in enthusiastic affirmation

Hoo-Poo Whereas high class personages smell fragrant like lotus flowers…
Hee-Pong Which he doesn't.

Dim Sum growls

Widow Twankee I see.
Hoo-Poo So… (*Like a quiz show host*) How do you pong? Doggy-doos or lotus flower?
Hee-Pong (*like a quiz show assistant*) Let's find out shall we? (*Lifting Dim Sum out of his basket*)
Widow Twankee 'Ere! Gerroff!

Dim Sum sniffs. Yowls. Keels over

Hee-Pong Hey! What you done to my doggy? (*He cradles the limp Dim Sum in his hands, then shrugging, slings the defunct puppet offstage by one ear*)
Hoo-Poo Quick — arrest her!
Hee-Pong Arrest her? But we want her gone.
Hoo-Poo Oh yeah… (*To Widow Twankee*) You! This time, just a caution. Now waddle off. Chop-chop.
Widow Twankee Excuse me? Waddle off?
Hoo-Poo Look — just go will you?
Widow Twankee Why should I?
Hee-Pong (*looking offstage* L) Hoo-Poo, quickly!
Hoo-Poo Look, I give you fiver to get lost.
Widow Twankee Make it a tenner.
Hoo-Poo Done.
Widow Twankee You have been.

They shake hands

Hee-Pong Hoo-Poo!

There is a loud dong from a huge gong somewhere nearby

Too late!

Act I, Scene 1

The Grand Vizier enters L, followed by an attendant

Hoo-Poo (*hissing to Widow Twankee*) Stand there. Say nothing.

Hoo-Poo and Hee-Pong stand shoulder to shoulder between Widow Twankee and the Grand Vizier, in an attempt to stop him seeing her

The Grand Vizier Make way! Make way!
Hee-Pong We've done that bit.
The Grand Vizier Oh. Right. And have you done a thorough sweep?
Hoo-Poo Yep.
The Grand Vizier Sniffer dog?
Hee-Pong Check.
Hoo-Poo Nothing to report, master.
The Grand Vizier Excellent. I shall signal the Imperial cavalcade that the route to the bath house has been cleared of common scum.
Hoo-Poo Hokey-kokey.

The Grand Vizier flicks a finger and sends his minion scurrying off

The Grand Vizier By the way… You'd better not have messed up this time. You know penalty for messing up?
Hoo-Poo }
Hee-Pong } (*together*) Head-chop!
The Grand Vizier Yes, head-chop. And you know penalty for common scum who lay unworthy eyes on Fragrant Imperial Scrumptiousness?
Hoo-Poo }
Hee-Pong } (*together*) Head-chop!
The Grand Vizier Correct! And you know penalty for police who mess up and allow common scum to lay unworthy eyes on Fragrant Imperial Scrumptiousness?

Hoo-Poo and Hee-Pong look uncertainly at each other, then venture

Hoo-Poo }
Hee-Pong } (*together*) Head-chop?
The Grand Vizier Wrong!

There is a tinkle on the cymbals as he indicates their lower anatomy… Hoo-Poo and Hee-Pong blanch and exchange pained looks

Hoo-Poo (*in a small voice*) Winky-chop?
The Grand Vizier (*with relish*) Winky-chop…

Both (*swallowing hard*) Ulp.
The Grand Vizier Wait!
Hoo-Poo What?!
The Grand Vizier (*pointing with his fan to Widow Twankee*) What is that?
Hoo-Poo (*pointing at Hee-Pong*) That?
The Grand Vizier (*waving Hee-Pong to one side and indicating Widow Twankee*) That.
Hoo-Poo (*feigning surprise*) Oh that… Yeah, well, that is a very noble…
Hee-Pong And not in least bit common…
Hoo-Poo …High class scrubber.
The Grand Vizier Is that right?
Widow Twankee I should cocoa. Pray h'allow me to h'introduce meself. Widow Twankee at your service, proprietress of the finest wet 'n' dry facility this side of Old Peking…
The Grand Vizier The Bath-house of Heavenly Delight I presume?
Widow Twankee No. The Happy Tub Chinese L——
Hoo-Poo (*interrupting*) YES!
Widow Twankee (*surprised*) Yes?
Hoo-Poo Yes! This Widow Twankee, keeper of delightful heavenly bath-house.
Widow Twankee Eh?
Hee-Pong Correct. She came to greet Fragrant Delectableness…
Hoo-Poo And take her back for a scrub.
Widow Twankee Now hang on a minute…
The Grand Vizier (*appalled*) A scrub?! Princess Jasmine does not scrub. Her divine body needs only the merest immersion in a tepid bath of pure spring water scented with rose petals.
Hoo-Poo Of course. Of course. Widow Twankee can oblige. Can't you?
Widow Twankee Can I?
Hoo-Poo (*pleading*) Say you can oblige…
Widow Twankee (*dubiously*) You're going to land me in a lot of trouble…
Hoo-Poo (*hissing*) You want we get winky-chop?!
Widow Twankee Bothered?
Hoo-Poo Listen. We make it worth your while.
Widow Twankee How?
Hoo-Poo We get you off any future climinal charge.
Hee-Pong For life.
Widow Twankee Anything?
Hoo-Poo Anything.

Act I, Scene 2

Widow Twankee Step this way, your immensity! The Delightfully Happy Tub of Heavenly Hygiene awaits its honourable royal occupant...

The Grand Vizier Excellent. Lead on...

Widow Twankee Adding rose petals to the water will make such a change from pee...

The Grand Vizier Pee?

Widow Twankee Yeah. Brings the whites up a treat doncha know... (*Taking him by the arm and leading him off, chattering*) Donkey pee is best, but I have been known to take a widdle in the tub meself...

Widow Twankee and The Grand Vizier exit

Hoo-Poo and Hee-Pong look at each other in horror, then run hell for leather in the opposite direction

The Lights fade

Scene 2

Mystical Eastern music. On the forestage area, the tent of Abanazar the Magician appears. Vaguely African — suggested by some vivid hanging fabric, animal skins and big pots...

Abanazar enters and addresses the audience

Abanazar Gold! Girls! Glory! In that order. It's not much to ask is it? I have plenty of gold of course — I am Abanazar, the greatest magician in all Africa — but I can't get enough of it, that's my problem. And as for girls and glory... Well, let's just say I've got a way to go... But my time will come — just you wait and see. Oh yes, my time will come by fair means or foul! Ha ha ha ha ha!!!

Audience participation

(*Leaning down to bait the audience*) Boo? Did somebody say boo? Am I supposed to be surprised or something? Look, excuse me for a moment would you? But I've just got to have a gloat... (*He rubs his hands together and chuckles horribly*)

A brief Black-out. With a loud bang and a blinding flash, the Slave of The Ring appears

(*Nearly jumping out of his skin; crossly*) Must you keep doing that?

The Slave of The Ring is huge, blue and very glittery — ideally he should wear a fake muscle suit beneath an open waistcoat, a big fancy turban, capacious pantaloons, and curly slippers

The Slave of The Ring (*intoning*) You summoned me, O Master?
Abanazar No — I was simply rubbing my hands in greedy anticipation. I must have accidentally rubbed my magic ring.
The Slave of The Ring Then I am yours to command.
Abanazar Well, since you're here, perhaps you could tell me how I can get my hands on more gold? Oh yes, and a beautiful girl... for I must tell you I have a long-felt ardour.
The Slave of The Ring (*cocking a sardonic eyebrow*) Really?
Abanazar (*irritably*) You're a genie — can't you just conjure these things from thin air?
The Slave of The Ring Alas, O Master, I am merely a lowly djinn of the third level. My genius is knowledge — not power. You need an all-powerful djinn of the seventh level.
Abanazar Then tell me where I can find such a being.
The Slave of The Ring The Slave of The Lamp is such a one...
Abanazar Ah — the fabled lamp. Oft we have spoken of this marvellous thing. But the lamp lies hidden in the Cave of a Thousand Rubies. It is death to enter there.
The Slave of The Ring Only for the fearful. But one without fear could win the lamp.
Abanazar Without fear? Ha! Impossible. Even the bravest of men knows fear. From the lowest mouse that creeps upon the sand, to the mightiest man of war, fear is handmaiden to survival.
The Slave of The Ring And yet to live in fear is a miserable condition.
Abanazar Look (*gesturing towards the audience*), if this lot wanted philosophy they could have stayed home and watched "The Simpsons". Get on with it...
The Slave of The Ring Very well. Know then, there *is* one without fear.
Abanazar Who?
The Slave of The Ring A boy.
Abanazar Where?
The Slave of The Ring In Old Peking, a thousand leagues hence.
Abanazar Near the Cave of the Rubies — what a coincidence — how is this boy called?
The Slave of The Ring He is named Aladdin.
Abanazar Beloved of Allah... But of course. (*Musing*) Do you have magic enough to take me there?

Act I, Scene 3

The Slave of The Ring (*none too certain*) Just about...
Abanazar Then do it.
The Slave of The Ring Your wish is my command, O wiliest of the wily. Shazzam! Abracadabra! And Kalamazoo!

Small pitiful puff of smoke. Nothing happens

Abanazar (*drily*) I'll fetch the camel, shall I?
The Slave of The Ring (*doubtfully*) It's an awfully long way...
Abanazar For gold, girls and glory it's no distance at all... Besides I have a few tricks of my own... (*He clicks his fingers*)

There is another brief Black-out and another flash – bigger! This time when the Lights come up, Abanazar has vanished

The Slave of The Ring (*looking decidedly miffed; crossly*) Oh bum!

He sidles off sheepishly

The Lights fade

Scene 3

To happy Chinese music, the main tabs open on to the Happy Tub Chinese Laundry. A sign overhead — or to one side — promotes the laundry and its work. Two loaded washing lines cross the width of the stage, each with a string of sheets, knickerbockers and other comic laundry items hanging from them. The front washing line has a large sheet hanging C *to obscure the giant wash tub which is set* C

Aladdin enters R, *peers at the audience, and then slaps his thigh*

Aladdin Hallo everyone — I'm Aladdin. Sorry I'm late. Had some important sleeping to catch up on...
Audience Oi Twankee!
Aladdin (*looking around*) She doesn't appear to be here, does she? Mum? Wishee-Washee? Where is everybody? I wonder where she's got to... (*He looks behind the big sheet hanging* C *on the front washing line*)

There is an instant squeal

(*Hastily pulling the sheet back into place and looking at the audience*)

Good grief. There's a girl in our tub... (*He takes another look behind the sheet*)

There is another immediate squeal

(*To the audience*) Quite a beautiful girl actually... And she hasn't got any clothes on.
Pianist Oh no there isn't!
Aladdin Oh yes there is. (*To audience*) Would you like to see?

Audience participation

That's a resounding yes from the men.

He pulls aside the big sheet to reveal the beautiful Princess Jasmine in the wash-tub. It's a big tub, so we can only see her head and bare shoulders

Hallo — who are you?
Princess Jasmine I might ask you the same question. How dare you intrude on a Princess's ablutions?!
Aladdin Wow! Are you a real Princess?
Princess Jasmine Yes. Now get out! And call me a rickshaw immediately.
Aladdin All right. You're a rickshaw.
Princess Jasmine Insolent jackal. Do you know who I am?
Aladdin No, but I'd like to.
Princess Jasmine (*imperiously*) I am Jasmine.
Aladdin Hallo Jasmine.
Princess Jasmine You're staring.
Aladdin I know.
Princess Jasmine Avert your eyes, and pass me a towel.

Aladdin offers a teeny flannel from the washing line

(*Glaring at him*) A bigger towel.
Aladdin Oh, sorry... (*He passes her a large fluffy bath towel from further down the line*)
Princess Jasmine Now if you wouldn't mind?

Aladdin draws the sheet across, so that she can climb out of the bath... After a moment, she comes out from between the hanging sheets, wrapped in the towel, or perhaps she has found a bathrobe or kimono somewhere

Act I, Scene 3

back there... She makes as if to continue drying herself, then pauses to glare at Aladdin who is still regarding her

Do you know the penalty for looking at me?
Aladdin (*cheerfully*) Haven't got a clue.
Princess Jasmine Head-chop.
Aladdin Wow. You mean I could lose my head just for looking at you?
Princess Jasmine Exactly.
Aladdin Well in that case I'd better take a really good look. (*He walks all the way around her, looking admiringly*)
Princess Jasmine (*waiting; one eyebrow cocked*) Well?
Aladdin Not bad…
Princess Jasmine (*unimpressed*) Thanks.
Aladdin Well, s'pose I'd better push off before your flunkeys come back. (*He turns to go*)
Princess Jasmine Wait. (*Intrigued; despite herself*) You haven't told me who you are…
Aladdin Oh — I'm Aladdin. This is my mother's laundry…
Princess Jasmine Laundry? Huh… Thought it was a bit crummy for a bath-house.
Aladdin Yeah, that's the soaking tub where we deal with particularly stubborn stains. (*He pulls the big hanging sheet* CR *off to one side to reveal the giant wash-tub again and to create some more space* C *for those who are to enter next*)
Princess Jasmine I can't believe I'm standing here talking to a wash-tub boy. You're just a little coolie.
Aladdin (*moving in on her*) Whereas you are a little hottie…
Princess Jasmine (*holding her ground*) You're rather forward.
Aladdin It's better than being a little backward… (*Abruptly, he turns to go*) Bye.
Princess Jasmine Wait! Come back immediately! (*Prettily stamping one small foot*) I order you!
Aladdin Ha! I'm Aladdin. Nobody orders me.
Princess Jasmine Oh… (*Perplexed*) Why aren't you afraid?
Aladdin I'm not afraid of anything… (*Slapping his thigh*) Actually though, I've decided to stay.
Princess Jasmine Why?
Aladdin Because I'm not sure I can take my eyes off you…
Princess Jasmine But it's against the law.
Aladdin I don't care.
Princess Jasmine You could lose your head.
Aladdin I already have.
Princess Jasmine Oh my. I think I like you.

Aladdin   I think I like you too.

> **Song 2** (Duet – Aladdin and Princess Jasmine)

At the end of the song they are about to kiss, when...

No-Lo-Fat   (*off*) JASMINE!
Aladdin   Who's that?!
Princess Jasmine   (*aghast*) My mother!
Aladdin   The Sultana?
Princess Jasmine   More like the whole fruit cake... Quick Aladdin, run! They must not find you with me.
Aladdin   All right — but I'll come and see you...
Princess Jasmine   (*horrified*) You cannot.
Aladdin   I've told you... Don't give me orders...

He steals a kiss and slips offstage R *just as the Herald of The Imperial Court enters* L

Herald   All quail before his Imperial Highness, Ming the Mirthless, Sultan of Ching-Chong, Ping-Pong, and Ooooagadoogoo, and his radiant Sultana, the beauteous No-Lo-Fat...

The Sultana, No-Lo-Fat and The Sultan, Ming the Mirthless enter L *followed by attendants including Pee-Long, Princess Jasmine's confidante. No-Lo-Fat is a huge, domineering woman. Ming the Mirthless her small, diffident, hen-pecked husband. No-Lo-Fat rushes over to Princess Jasmine and starts fussing*

No-Lo-Fat   Jasmine! Jasmine, my little egg noodle! What were those boneheads thinking of, leaving you in a place like this?
Princess Jasmine   I'm perfectly all right, Mother...
No-Lo-Fat   Don't be ridiculous! Of course you're not all right! On your own out here where (*glaring at the audience*) common people can look at you...
Princess Jasmine   (*wearily*) Nobody looked at me...
No-Lo-Fat   (*outraged*) You mean they ignored you?! The vile rabble! (*Rounding on Ming the Mirthless*) See what a worthless, mongrel people you rule over? This is what comes of being lax...
Ming the Mirthless   (*absently*) Yes dear...
No-Lo-Fat   (*to the Herald*) Execute every third person in the entire district!

Act I, Scene 3

The Herald signals an attendant, who makes to dart off but is forestalled by a cry from Princess Jasmine

Princess Jasmine No — wait! Look… Someone did talk to me — but you must promise not to be cross.
No-Lo-Fat (*innocence personified*) Cross? Moi?
Princess Jasmine Promise..?
No-Lo-Fat Promise.
Princess Jasmine Well there was this boy… He was very kind. And *very* handsome…
No-Lo-Fat (*containing herself with difficulty*) I see. What sort of boy?
Princess Jasmine A laundry boy.
No-Lo-Fat (*as Lady Bracknell*) A laundry boy? And does this handsome laundry boy have a name?
Princess Jasmine (*wistfully*) Aladdin.
No-Lo-Fat (*to herself*) Aladdin… (*Pause, then screaming*) OFF WITH HIS HEAD!

Attendants rush off in all directions

Princess Jasmine But you promised you wouldn't be cross!
No-Lo-Fat Cross? I'm not cross — I'm absolutely livid! I'm spitting teeth! You talked to a laundry boy?!! OHHHH the shame of it! (*Rounding on Ming the Mirthless again*) I warned you, didn't I?! I told you that Grand Vizier was a complete waste of space.
Ming the Mirthless Yes dear.
No-Lo-Fat But would you listen? Would you?
Ming the Mirthless No dear.
No-Lo-Fat But I was right, wasn't I?
Ming the Mirthless Three bags full dear.
No-Lo-Fat Don't be impertinent!
Ming the Mirthless No dear. Sorry dear.
No-Lo-Fat That's better. (*To attendants*) Bring in the Grand Vizier.

Hoo-Poo and Hee-Pong – carrying foam rubber truncheons – enter with the Grand Vizier, who is flung to the floor

The Grand Vizier Highness, your unworthy servant abases himself before you. I ——
No-Lo-Fat Silence, you snivelling cur! You brought my precious daughter to this festering sewer to bathe in a common wash-tub?!
The Grand Vizier Mercy Highness! It wasn't my fault… It was these two ——

But before he can shift the blame, Hoo-Poo and Hee-Pong fall upon the Grand Vizier and belabour him furiously with their foam rubber truncheons

Hoo-Poo (*screaming*) Silence! No answer back Sultana, rudesby!
Hee-Pong Speak only when spoken to...
No-Lo-Fat Enough! (*Leaning down to coo in the Grand Vizier's ear*) Not your fault? When every fool in Peking knows that the Bath-house of Heavenly Delight is on the Avenue of Celestial Peach Blossom...
The Grand Vizier Yes Highness...
No-Lo-Fat As opposed to this... establishment... Which is where?
The Grand Vizier (*mumbling*) The Back Alley of Reeking Effluent, Highness...
No-Lo-Fat Exactly. The Back Alley of Reeking Peking Effluent! Do you know, Grand Vizier, the penalty for messing up?
The Grand Vizier (*miserably*) Head-chop?
No-Lo-Fat Quite so. (*Bellowing*) Chip-Chop-Ow!

Sinister chords. A huge bald executioner enters, big gleaming chopper over his shoulder

Everyone else on stage looks deeply uncomfortable and edges slightly away from him

The Grand Vizier No! Mercy! Please!
Ming the Mirthless (*intervening*) Erm... Aren't you being a little hasty, dear? I mean he is quite useful after all... Prime Minister, Chancellor of the Exchequer, takes back the empties — that sort of thing...
No-Lo-Fat (*irritably*) Oh very well... Sentence commuted.
The Grand Vizier (*collapsing*) Oh thank heavens...
No-Lo-Fat Winky-chop.
The Grand Vizier Noooooooooooo!

Chip-Chop-Ow produces an ice cream scoop or other inappropriate surgical instrument

Ming the Mirthless Look, how about a pigtail-chop?
No-Lo-Fat (*miffed*) Oh all right.
The Grand Vizier No! No! Not my pigtail! Oh the humiliation...
No-Lo-Fat Chip-Chop-Ow.

The Grand Vizier is hauled to his feet by Hoo-Poo and Hee-Pong and turned so that his back is to the audience. The huge executioner steps

Act I, Scene 3

forward, produces a tiny pair of nail scissors, and there is a tinny "snip" as the Grand Vizier's pigtail is cruelly amputated

Take him away...

The sobbing Grand Vizier is dragged off by attendants

(*Turning her glare on to Hoo-Poo and Hee-Pong*) Now — you two clowns — find this Aladdin. And when you do, take him straight to Chip-Chop-Ow.

Hoo-Poo and Hee-Pong snap to attention and then turn to go. Then Hoo-Poo remembers something and turns back. Hee-Pong turns back too, but unfortunately straight into a pair of voluminous knickers hanging from the washing line, where he is obliged to stand while Hoo-Poo asks...

Hoo-Poo Head-chop?
No-Lo-Fat Everything chop! The lot! (*Lifting the knickers from Hee-Pong's face and glaring at him*) Head last...

Hoo-Poo and Hee-Pong turn again, and this time they do go off

Princess Jasmine (*horrified*) Mother — no!
No-Lo-Fat And as you can't be trusted, my girl, I shall leave my executioner here to make sure you don't get into any more mischief. I'll see you back at the palace.

No-Lo-Fat sweeps off

Ming the Mirthless (*absently*) Cheerio dear...
Princess Jasmine Bye Dad.

Ming the Mirthless smiles hesitantly then wanders off after No-Lo-Fat, followed by attendants

Pee-Long bows as they all exit, then crosses to Princess Jasmine

Pee-Long Oh Mistress... I knew I should have come with you. Are you all right?
Princess Jasmine Oh Pee-Long. (*Suddenly noticing that Chip-Chop-Ow is still there*) Wait outside slave!

The inscrutable Chip-Chop-Ow bows and exits

Pee-Long What is it Mistress?
Princess Jasmine I don't want Aladdin to get the chop.
Pee-Long But he looked at you.
Princess Jasmine I know he did. And I liked it.
Pee-Long (*shocked*) Mistress! (*Pause*) Tell me all about it. What was he like?
Princess Jasmine Oh, he's the most beautiful boy I've ever seen.
Pee-Long (*frowning*) He's the only boy you've ever seen.
Princess Jasmine Yes, I know… I think it must be love.
Pee-Long Beansprouts! That's bad.
Princess Jasmine And now they're going to lop his pretty head off.
Pee-Long Oh well… Plenty more fish in the sea.
Princess Jasmine (*fiercely*) No! We must find him before they do.
Pee-Long But you can't go wandering the streets — you're a Princess.
Princess Jasmine Then you'll have to do it. You can go anywhere.
Pee-Long But I don't know what he looks like.
Princess Jasmine Oh that's easy, he's the principal boy: Tall, slim and foxy as hell. Tunic, long boots, slaps his thigh a lot. Like this… (*She slaps*)
Pee-Long Not like this? (*She slaps*)
Princess Jasmine No, like this… (*She slaps*)

They both pause, wince, and rub their thighs

Pee-Long Right — I'll see what I can do.
Princess Jasmine (*taking Pee-Long by the shoulders and shaking her to and fro*) Pee-Long, you must find him! I'll kill myself before I'd let anything happen to Aladdin. I can't live without him… (*She rushes sobbing to one side of the stage*)
Pee-Long (*irritated; following her*) Oh for Heaven's sake, stop being such a drama queen.
Princess Jasmine Hallo? I'm a Princess.
Pee-Long Oh yes. Sorry…
Princess Jasmine (*rhetorically*) Oh Aladdin… Where are you now…?

The Lights fade. Music

Act I, Scene 4

Scene 4

Before the main tabs. Aladdin enters and speaks to the audience

Aladdin Hallo again. Have you seen my Mum recently? I can't wait to tell her about Princess Jasmine…

Hee-Pong can be heard making nee-naw noises offstage

Oops, I think someone's coming… Better make myself scarce…

He hides just as Hoo-Poo and Hee-Pong enter

Ideally this should be from somewhere unexpected, like the rear of the auditorium, and preferably they should be on wheels — scooters are ideal. There is a major cacophony as Hoo-Poo whistles and Hee-Pong nee-naws

Business with the audience as they park their scooters and ascend the stage. Then sound effect of hammering as — completely out of time — Hoo-Poo uses a foam rubber mallet to mime hammering up a wanted poster on the Proscenium arch… Unable to reconcile the random hammering sound effects with his hammering movements, Hoo-Poo regards the mallet in his hand with annoyance, then tries it out by hitting Hee-Pong over the head with it. Eventually, the hammering sound effects cease and Hoo-Poo steps back to admire his handiwork

Hoo-Poo (*proclaiming*) Wanted, dead or alive…
Hee-Pong — but preferably alive so that the Sultana can kill him slowly…
Hoo-Poo …Aladdin, son of Widow Twankee of the Happy Tub Chinese Laundry. For casting his worthless eyes on Her Fragrant Delectableness, Jasmine, daughter of his Imperial Immensity, Ming the Mirthless, Sultan of Ching-Chong, Ping-Pong, and Oooooagadoogoo…
Hee-Pong Reward: Ten trillion nik-niks.
Hoo-Poo Which is about twenty-seven pence.
Hee-Pong (*to audience*) So, have you lot seen him?

Audience participation

Hoo-Poo I think you have.

Audience participation

Oh yes you have...

Audience participation

I think you're telling porkies.
Hee-Pong Yeah! Double-cooked porkies in fibbing sauce.
Hoo-Poo Yeah! You just a bunch of fibbers.
Hee-Pong Hmmm... (*Reflectively, rubbing his tummy*) Fibbing sauce... That reminds me Hoo-Poo... I hungry...
Hoo-Poo Hokai — fine. Whatchoo want? Pizza? Indian?
Hee-Pong No — don' be silly... (*Beaming*) I like Chinese!

Song 3 (Hoo-Poo and Hee-Pong)

(*After the song, addressing the audience*) Hokai... You lot better watch your step... It velly serious offence you know — aiding and abetting known climinal...
Hoo-Poo Yeah — just you watch it, that's all... Come on, Hee-Pong, let's keep looking...

They go down and collect their scooters then exit the way the came in, making siren noises as they go... Once the "nee-naws" have faded into the distance, Widow Twankee wanders on to the forestage area

Widow Twankee Oh the news is all over the place! It's all gone 'orribly wrong, and it's all my fault...
Aladdin (*emerging from his hiding place*) Have they gone?
Widow Twankee Aladdin — there you are!
Aladdin Mum, wonderful news! I met a girl...
Widow Twankee Yes, I know you did.
Aladdin She's a Princess...
Widow Twankee Yes, I know she is.
Aladdin I think I'm in love with her...
Widow Twankee Yes, I know you — (*amazed*) are you?
Aladdin Yep. And I'm going to marry her and live happily ever after.
Widow Twankee (*grimly*) Oh no you're not.
Aladdin Oh yes I am. Why shouldn't I?
Widow Twankee Because they're going to chop your noddle off you great 'nana!
Aladdin Don't be ridiculous. Of course they're not. (*Pause*) ...Are they?

Act I, Scene 4

Widow Twankee You need to get out of town, my lad.
Aladdin Impossible. I have work to do.
Widow Twankee (*aside*) Well that'll be a first.
Aladdin I need to make enough money to become posh. Then I can ask the Sultan for his daughter's hand in marriage.
Widow Twankee Well — it's a plan... But until then, we need to save your neck... (*Thinking for a moment*) I've got it: you must disguise yourself...
Aladdin What? But I'm the principal boy. I'll stick out like a sore thumb.
Widow Twankee Ah, no, that's just it, you see. There's another principal boy in town...
Aladdin There is? Who?
Widow Twankee Sinbad.
Aladdin What — the sailor?
Widow Twankee That's him. So, you can disguise yourself as him until all this fuss blows over.
Aladdin How am I going to do that?
Widow Twankee Peasy... (*Removing Aladdin's coolie hat, rummaging in her handbag and putting an improvised turban on him*) Sorted. Now say aah...
Aladdin Aaah.
Widow Twankee And again.
Aladdin Aaah. Aaah.
Widow Twankee Keep it going...
Aladdin Aaaah. Aaaah. Aaaar. Aaaarrrr...
Widow Twankee There you go — Sinbad the Sailor...
Aladdin Brilliant.
Widow Twankee Right. I'm off down the laundry to kick-start Wishee-Washee. See you later...
Aladdin Mum?
Widow Twankee What?
Aladdin Thanks.
Widow Twankee Don't mention it.

Widow Twankee exits

Song 4 (Aladdin)

At the end of the song, Abanazar enters, his magician's finery concealed beneath a plain cloak

Abanazar Salaam young master...

Audience participation

(*Coming down to the audience; forcing politeness*) Look, if you wouldn't mind? I'm trying to perpetrate a deception here, so do you think you could just pipe down a bit before I turn you all into frogspawn? Thank you so much...

Aladdin Hallo. Can I help you?

Abanazar Yes... I'm looking for Aladdin.

Aladdin Never heard of him.

Abanazar Ah. Might I enquire as to your name?

Aladdin Sinbad.

Abanazar (*dubiously*) Really?

Aladdin Aaah. Aaah.

Abanazar (*puzzled*) Sinbad the seagull?

Aladdin No, listen... Aaaah-Aaaah. Arrrr.

Abanazar Oh yes, of course — Sinbad the Sailor... Pity. I had hoped you were Aladdin. What a shame...

Aladdin Why?

Abanazar Because I am going to make Aladdin an offer he can't refuse — the chance to make his fortune!

Aladdin Wow! In that case — I am Aladdin.

Abanazar Really? You're not Sinbad then?

Aladdin No. Look. (*He swaps his turban for his coolie hat, and then back again*) Ta-daaa!

Abanazar (*delighted*) Of course — I see it now! Come, let me smother you in kisses...

Aladdin I'm sorry?

Abanazar Aladdin — my long-lost nephew! Come to your old Uncle Abanazar... Let me embrace you...

Aladdin Uncle?

Abanazar (*snapping*) Yes Uncle. Of course Uncle... (*Recovering his poise*) Don't tell me your dear mother has never talked about her favourite brother-in-law?

Aladdin Erm, no...

Abanazar Oh well, never mind. Let me look at you... Yes, you're the absolute spit of your father...

Aladdin That's funny. 'Cos I was adopted.

Abanazar (*improvising*) So was he! There — see how alike you are? Now your father and I... (*Pause*) What was his name again...?

Aladdin Neville...

Abanazar Yes, we were like two peas in a bucket, Nev and I... I can't believe your mother never mentioned me...

Aladdin Well if she did, I don't remember it ...

Act I, Scene 5

Abanazar Not a problem. Tell you what, here are ten silver dinars — a token of my good faith. (*He hands over a small purse of money*)
Aladdin Blimey.
Abanazar Are you sure you don't remember?
Aladdin Actually, it's starting to come back to me...
Abanazar Excellent! I knew it would. Now tell me, wouldn't you like to make some serious money?
Aladdin Yep — but that tends to involve serious work, and work and I don't get on...
Abanazar My boy, I know exactly what you mean. But what if I could show you how to get rich quick with hardly any work at all?
Aladdin That'd be all right. I could do with the dosh. I need to make enough to ask the Sultan for Princess Jasmine's hand in marriage.
Abanazar Really? Well come with me now, and we'll make a start right away...
Aladdin Erm, well I ought to let Mum know where I'm going first. Besides, you'll be wanting to say hallo, won't you?
Abanazar I'm sorry?
Aladdin To catch up on old times?
Abanazar Er, well, yes, obviously — but...
Aladdin Well come on then...
Abanazar Oh, er.. right, yes. So... tell me about this princess of yours... Is she beautiful? Is she game? And just as important — is she wealthy...?

They exit

The Lights fade

Scene 5

A clearing

Lights come up to a spooky greeny-blue

Silver shimmers across the bare stage. Mysterious oriental music — like the "Singapore" theme from "Pirates of The Caribbean: At World's End" — tinkles in the twilight. Shadowy figures flit across the stage, clearly up to no good... When the music changes to the loud bit, the stage suddenly erupts with as many villainous Chinese pirates as can be gathered. They are all armed to the teeth and have long moustaches — including the women and children. They do cartwheels and handsprings, then race about the stage in time to the music, searching. It's really quite spectacular

Abruptly, a sinister gong sounds, and Mrs Cheng enters... a diminutive Chinese lady in traditional dress. She has devilish curly fingernails. She doesn't look dangerous, but is actually quite terrifying

Mrs Cheng Well, my floating filth of the Yangtse Delta — what news? Have you found Sinbad the Sailor for me? ...Nip-Tuk?
Nip-Tuk We've ransacked every sampan on the Yellow River. Not a sign of him.
Mrs Cheng Wong-Ki-I?
Wong-Ki-I We've scoured every street from Choo-Ching-Chow to Chow-Ching-Chong... Nothing.
Mrs Cheng Kung Po Prawn?
Kung Po Prawn We've searched every inch of the Imperial Pleasure Gardens and the Summer Palace...
Nip-Tuk Where twice five miles of fertile ground with walls and towers are girdled round...
Wong-Ki-I And there are gardens bright with sinuous rills, where blossoms many an incense-bearing tree...
Kung Po Prawn And here were forests —
Mrs Cheng (*interrupting*) STOP! Stop right now with the versification! You're supposed to be vicious cutthroat scum, not pansy poets!
Crew Oh yes. Harr harr. Scurvy dog. Bilge rats. Pieces of eight. Sorry. Etc.
Mrs Cheng Wong-Wei?
Wong-Wei Yah?
Mrs Cheng Did you find Sinbad?
Wong-Wei Nah.
Mrs Cheng Why not?
Wong-Wei Wong-Wei go wrong way.
Mrs Cheng I see... (*To Nip-Tuk*) Kill him.

The other pirates close in on Wong-Wei with daggers drawn

Wong-Wei No — stop! Wong-Wei find something velly interesting instead...
Mrs Cheng Speak.
Wong-Wei Abanazar the Gleat is in Peking...
Kung Po Prawn Yah! Disguised as kindly old buffer...
Mrs Cheng Abanazar?
Nip-Tuk The pantomime villain.
Mrs Cheng Pantomime villain? (*Sneering*) He's not a pantomime villain... *I* am a pantomime villain! Mwoah —hahahahaha!!!!

Act I, Scene 5

Lights change. Thunder crashes and lightning splits the sky. Captain Nemo organ music is heard. Mrs Cheng suddenly seems to swell into a much larger figure of evil

Crew (*together*) Mwoah-hahahahaha!!!!

Lights back to normal. The moment passes. Mrs Cheng is just a diminutive Chinese lady again

Mrs Cheng Abanazar is a mountebank — a tuppenny conjuror... Forget him. Find Sinbad! Turn this crawling dungheap of a city upside down! Slit a thousand throats if you have to — but bring me that boy! (*Distantly*) ...He has something dear to me...

The Pirates all gather into a huddle and whisper to each other, trying to work out what Sinbad has stolen from Mrs Cheng. They all look up, then back into the huddle again. There is a bit of jostling and then Wong-Wei gets pushed forward. The others signal to him to speak

Wong-Wei (*nervously*) Mrs Cheng, sir...
Mrs Cheng What?
Wong-Wei Is it your disembodied heart beating inside a wooden box?
Crew (*awestruck*) Ahhhhhhhhhhhhhhhhhhh...
Mrs Cheng Don't be so ridiculous... (*Pause*) It is *much* more precious than that. And once I have recovered it, I will flay the thief Sinbad alive, and use his skin as toilet paper.
Crew (*roaring in approval*) Aaaahhhhhhhhhhhhhhhhh...
Mrs Cheng Now I don't care how you do it — but (*shouting*) bring me Sinbad the Sailor!

Song 5 (The Pirates)

At the end of the song they disperse, villainously through the audience, terrorising the people sitting on the aisles

Lights fade. There is jolly Chinese music to cover the short scene change required to the set

Scene 6

The Happy Tub laundry. A table and chairs are set for tea... One of the washing lines is still up, but the wash-tub has gone. Widow Twankee is just taking down some washing and handing it to Wishee-Washee when Aladdin enters, Abanazar trailing behind him

Aladdin Mother...
Widow Twankee Aladdin — there you are. How's the disguise going?
Aladdin Works a treat. But never mind that... Look who I've brought to see you...
Widow Twankee (*peering hard at Abanazar*) Good grief! It's not is it?
Aladdin (*beaming*) It is...
Widow Twankee You've found him after all these years...
Abanazar What?
Widow Twankee (*to the audience*) It's Osama Bin Laden.
Aladdin No, silly... It's Uncle Abanazar. (*He goes to sit at the table and help himself to tea*)
Widow Twankee Oh yes, of course it is... Abanazar you old goat, how are you? What have you been up to, and — (*Pause*) Hang on a tick. (*Turning to Aladdin*) You don't have an Uncle Abanazar...
Abanazar (*quickly*) O Sister-in-law. Don't say you've forgotten me as well? And after I've come all this way to make you rich.
Widow Twankee Rich? Rich? Well why didn't you say so? ...How rich?
Abanazar Beyond your wildest dreams. And it begins here. This golden bracelet is my gift to you, O wife of my late lamented brother. (*He hands her some trinket*)
Widow Twankee Aladdin, shift your butt. Let your Uncle Abanazar park his bum. (*To Abanazar*) Tea?
Wishee-Washee Hey! You just say he no havee Nuncle Nabanazar...
Widow Twankee (*aside*) Everyone needs an Uncle Abanazar. If he's handing out the bling, he can be my Great-Aunt Fanny if he wants. I'm not complaining.

Widow Twankee and Abanazar are now sitting either side of the table, with Wishee-Washee and Aladdin standing behind them

(*To Abanazar; offering sugar*) Two lumps?
Abanazar Yes, I can see...
Wishee-Washee But —
Widow Twankee (*rounding on Wishee-Washee*) Look, Wishee-Washee — what have we got?

Act I, Scene 6

Wishee-Washee Nuttin'.
Widow Twankee Exactly — so what he can possibly want from us? Nothing. How can we lose? (*To Abanazar again; now in her best posh voice*) So tell me, have you come far?
Abanazar Africa.
Widow Twankee (*still posh*) Oh, quite local then?
Abanazar (*ignoring her*) Let me come straight to the point.

As one, the three of them make an exaggerated move to lean in and listen intently to him... Abanazar regards them in slight alarm he soldiers on

> This very night, I have a task to undertake. If all goes well, my fortune will be made forever – and yours. For I am willing to share my booty with you, my dear long-lost family...

As one, the three of them look down to where he has one curly-toed boot thrust forward... Abanazar regards them with ill-concealed contempt. Clearly they are idiots

> No, no... My booty — you know, like treasure... I will share it with you, if you will but assist me in the venture...

Widow Twankee Well, yes — of course — please — definitely — how?
Abanazar Only one who is without fear will be of use to me in this night's work. One who is agile and strong; honest and true of heart.
Widow Twankee Well that's me out... (*Sudden idea*) Ooooh — I know! How about Aladdin?
Abanazar The boy? (*Feigning doubt*) Is he honest? Is he brave?
Widow Twankee Brave? Ha! He doesn't know the meaning of the word fear... (*To Aladdin*) "Fear".

Wishee-Washee jumps slightly in alarm, but Aladdin just looks puzzled

Aladdin What does that mean?
Widow Twankee (*to Abanazar*) See?
Abanazar Very well... Know then...

Abanazar stalks D, declaiming, with the three of them following, matching him step for step

> ...That not many leagues from this place, beneath the shadow of the Iron Mountain, I have discovered a secret cavern — the Cave of a Thousand Rubies...

Widow Twankee Ooooooooooooooooh... (*A beat*) And what's inside?

Abanazar (*stunned by her stupidity; pulling an expression of disbelief*) Well durr — rubies, obviously... Not to mention untold gold and precious jewels. Fabulous wealth beyond the imagining of man.
Widow Twankee And you'll share it with us?
Abanazar My word on it.
Widow Twankee Well, I don't know... Sounds a bit too good to be true... I mean, I don't know whether we can trust you... (*To the audience*) What do you lot think — should we trust him?

Audience participation

(*Appearing to listen, then turning back to Abanazar*) They said yes we should — considering how much money is at stake.
Abanazar Excellent! (*Turning to Aladdin, he claps one hand on his shoulder in a hail-fellow-well-met kind of way*) Well Aladdin — will you come with your Uncle Abanazar to unlock the secrets of the Cave of a Thousand Rubies? What do you say?

Aladdin responds by mirroring Abanazar's gesture and clapping one hand on Abanazar's shoulder. Which makes Abanazar deeply uncomfortable

Aladdin I say try and stop me! (*He slaps his thigh*)
Abanazar Ha ha ha ha ha... That's the spirit... (*Squirming away from beneath Aladdin's honest, manly grip on his shoulder*) You're a chip off the old block all right... (*He feigns a frat-boy play punch to Aladdin's arm*)

Aladdin laughs and again responds in kind — only he delivers a whopping great punch to Abanazar's bicep, causing Abanazar to grip his upper arm and bend double with a silent scream of pain

Abruptly, the sound of nee-nawing can be heard somewhere in the distance

Wishee-Washee Listen — what that?

Distant nee-naws getting louder

Aladdin The police!
Widow Twankee Run for it!
Abanazar Er... Do we have a problem here?
Widow Twankee No, no... Just a little misunderstanding that's all.

Act I, Scene 6

There is a hammering on the door L, Wishee-Washee rushes to hide under a table — his quivering bottom facing the audience

The Grand Vizier (*off*) Open up! In the name of his Imperial Immensity, Ming the Mirthless, Sultan of Ching-Chong, Ping-Pong, and Oooooagadoogoo…
Widow Twankee Right. Out the back… (*She chivvies Abanazar and Aladdin offstage R*)
Abanazar Yes but — I…
Widow Twankee No buts. Out you go.
The Grand Vizier (*off*) Open the door or we'll break it down!
Widow Twankee (*shouting*) I wouldn't do that if I were you — it's the only thing that's holding the set up.
Aladdin Goodbye Mother — I shall return a wealthy man…
Widow Twankee Good for you. But if you don't get out now, you'll be a dead one first.

Aladdin and a flustered Abanazar exit R

Widow Twankee hauls Wishee-Washee out from his hiding place and pushes him over to open the door L

Wishee-Washee — door.

Wishee-Washee opens the door to admit the Grand Vizier, Chip-Chop-Ow, Hoo-Poo and Hee-Pong

Hallo — if you're selling *Amway*, I've already got a shedload of detergent.
The Grand Vizier (*screaming*) Silence scum! Knock head!
Widow Twankee If you insist… (*She raps him briskly on the forehead — tok-tok-tok*)
The Grand Vizier No! Knock head on floor, pig. Kow-Tow! Kow-Tow!
Widow Twankee I'm not kow-towing to anybody, pal.

No-Lo-Fat sweeps on, hoiking the Grand Vizier back out of the way

No-Lo-Fat Out of my way, worm.
Widow Twankee You tell him, love…
No-Lo-Fat (*to Widow Twankee*) Do you know who I am?
Widow Twankee Are you Bernard Manning's body double? (*Or substitute other well-known rotund person*)
No-Lo-Fat No-Lo-Fat.

Widow Twankee Yes I can tell.
No-Lo-Fat Your Sultana.
Widow Twankee Plump but slightly wrinkled.
No-Lo-Fat I beg your pardon?
Widow Twankee Granted.
No-Lo-Fat You are Widow Twankee?
Widow Twankee Might be.
No-Lo-Fat Where is your son, Aladdin?
Widow Twankee Haven't seen him for days.
No-Lo-Fat (*to her minions*) Search the place.
Widow Twankee What's he supposed to have done anyhow?
No-Lo-Fat He laid his unworthy eyes on my precious daughter.
Widow Twankee Disgraceful. I hope you told her off.

Following a very desultory search, The Grand Vizier, Hoo-Poo and Hee-Pong exchange shrugs

Grand Vizier The boy Aladdin is not here, Highness.
No-Lo-Fat Very well. In that case... (*pointing to Widow Twankee*) take her.
Widow Twankee Ooooh I say!
Hoo-Poo Come on you...
Widow Twankee Where are we going?
Hoo-Poo Jail.

They lay hold of her... Chip-Chop-Ow produces an incongrous expanding tape measure and starts taking neck and other sinister measurements

Widow Twankee Jail? Jail? But I've done nothing wrong! (*Melodramatically*) I am an innocent man!

Pause. They all stare at her

  (*Embarrassed; correcting herself*) Woman. Help! Wishee-Washee!

Wishee-Washee dutifully scampers up to assist — but is held off easily by Hee-Pong with one big hand placed on Wishee-Washee's forehead. Wishee-Washee runs on the spot until he eventually tires and stops. Whereupon Hee-Pong bops him on the head with his truncheon, and Wishee-Washee collapses on to the floor in a heap

No-Lo-Fat As I can't execute your son, I will have to execute you instead. If Aladdin gives himself up by dawn tomorrow, you live. If not...

Act I, Scene 7

All (*leering*) Head-chop...
No-Lo-Fat (*to Wishee-Washee*) You — slave. Spread the word.
Wishee-Washee No! Widow Twankeeeeeeeeeeeeeeeeeeeeeee!!!!

Widow Twankee is marched out. Exit all except Wishee-Washee who sits on the floor and starts bawling like a baby

The Lights fade

Scene 7

In front of the main tabs... A street in Old Peking. Sinbad enters L

Sinbad (*to the audience*) Mrs Cheng's agents are everywhere. I can trust nobody in this strange city. I must assume a cunning disguise. (*Throwing away his turban and popping on a coolie hat*) There. Now I blend in. Ha! (*He slaps his thigh*)

Pee-Long enters R

Pee-Long Do that again.
Sinbad I'm sorry?
Pee-Long That thing you just did. Do it again.
Sinbad What this? (*He slaps his thigh again*)
Pee-Long It's you, isn't it?
Sinbad No, it's not.
Pee-Long Yes it is. You're the principal boy, aren't you?
Sinbad (*uncertain where this is going*) Well, yes I am, but...
Pee-Long My Mistress was right. You're very handsome.
Sinbad Your Mistress? Not Mrs Cheng by any chance?
Pee-Long No, Princess Jasmine, silly...
Sinbad (*confused*) I don't know any Princess Jasmine.
Pee-Long Oh it's all right, you don't have to pretend with me. I know all about it.
Sinbad I don't have a clue what you're talking about. (*Pause*) Look, I don't suppose you'd like to hear about my seven incredible voyages, would you?
Pee-Long Oh yes please.
Sinbad Very well. I'll tell you in exchange for a kiss.
Pee-Long All right then.

They go to kiss. At which point Hoo-Poo and Hee-Pong run on

Hoo-Poo Hold it!

They are now armed with foam rubber nunchuks, and strike silly martial arts poses holding their nunchuks aloft. Unfortunately, Hee-Pong, who is behind Hoo-Poo, lets his nunchuk slip and one end flicks forward and bops Hoo-Poo on the head. Hoo-Poo turns and glares at Hee-Pong. Hee-Pong looks shamefaced, and replaces his nunchuks in his belt

Sinbad What's the matter?
Hoo-Poo You must be Aladdin.
Sinbad Er... (*Hastily*) Yes! Yes I am. That's exactly who I am. Aladdin.
Pee-Long I knew it...
Hee-Pong Excellent! You nicked. (*They slap the cuffs on Sinbad*)
Sinbad What?!
Hoo-Poo (*pointing to the wanted poster still pinned to the proscenium arch*) You common scum that laid unworthy eyes on Fragrant Imperial Scrumptiousness...
Hee-Pong Penalty: Head-chop.
Sinbad Head-chop? Just for looking? Well I hope she was worth it...
Hee-Pong Count yourself lucky it not winky-chop...
Sinbad (*aside to the audience*) That might be difficult...
Hoo-Pong Come on.
Sinbad (*to Pee-Long*) Well bye then... Don't forget you owe me a kiss...

They drag him off

Pee-Long Oh Heavens — now what am I going to do? My Mistress is in love with him. And I think I might be too! But unless we can save him from Chip-Chop-Ow, neither of us will have him.

She scuttles off

The Lights fade

Scene 8

Outside The Cave of a Thousand Rubies

Abanazar and Aladdin enter. Aladdin carries a coil of stout rope over one shoulder

Aladdin The Iron Mountain... Is this it?
Abanazar Yes... It's round here somewhere. The entrance must be concealed. I shall need a little expert assistance to find it.
Aladdin Satnav?
Abanazar Oh much better than that... How would you like to rub my ring?
Aladdin No thanks Uncle — I'm fine really. But you go ahead...
Abanazar Do you like it? (*Showing it off*) It's solid gold... Ying-and-Yang...
Aladdin Nice.
Abanazar More than nice. Observe... (*He rubs his magic ring*)

There is a brief Black-out and a flash

The Slave of The Ring appears

The Slave of The Ring You summoned me, O Master?
Abanazar For once — yes.
Aladdin Wow — a genie!
Abanazar Answer me — where lies The Cave of a Thousand Rubies?
The Slave of The Ring Behind yonder rock.
Abanazar And how does it open?
The Slave of The Ring Just say the magic word.
Abanazar Open Sesame?
The Slave of The Ring Wrong.
Abanazar Hocus Pocus!
The Slave of The Ring Nope.
Abanazar Abracadabra?

The Slave of The Ring shakes his head

  Erm... "Izzy-Wizzy, Let's Get Busy!"
The Slave of The Ring No. Come on, it's easy... (*To the audience*) What's the magic word children?

Audience participation

Abanazar (*in disgust*) "Please"?
The Slave of The Ring That's it. The magic word.
Abanazar But I *hate* saying please...

The Slave of The Ring shrugs. Muttering darkly, Abanazar crosses to stand by the wall of rock

Oh all right... Open — (*whining voice*) — please?

There is a creaking, graunching rumble as the cave opens to reveal a narrow fissure in the rock face, just wide enough for a slim person to climb through

There — The Cave of a Thousand Rubies! (*To Aladdin*) You must climb through and down into the chamber.
Aladdin Me? Aren't you coming too?
Abanazar Alas, I am too broad to pass through the entrance... Nor nimble enough to make the descent. I will make fast the rope. You alone must enter.
Aladdin All right, I will. (*He busies himself tying the rope around his middle*)
Abanazar Good boy... Inside, you will find dazzling riches. But first you must locate an old lamp. It will be set in some niche or cranny. Find it and bring it to me. Then return and fill your boots with rubies and diamonds. Live like a Prince for eternity!
Aladdin You don't need to tell me twice! (*He starts to climb in*)
Abanazar That's my boy... Now don't forget — bring me the lamp first.
Aladdin (*pausing*) What, ahead of bagfuls of rubies and golden treasure?
Abanazar Patience, Aladdin, is a virtue. The lamp is precious to me... Worthless — but of sentimental value...
Aladdin All right. If I can see it... (*He starts to climb in again*)
Abanazar Aladdin — one more thing. There are perils within. Evil spirits will seek to terrify you and drive you to insanity. It is death to fear them. Death to flee.
Aladdin I'm not scared of ghosts.
Abanazar Right answer... In you go then, quickly. And pass me the lamp as soon as you can.
Aladdin Er... You won't let go of the rope will you?
Abanazar (*wounded*) As if!

Aladdin disappears into the crack

Act I, Scene 9

>(*Turning to The Slave of The Ring*) You were right. The boy has no fear...
>**The Slave of The Ring** If he had, he would know you have already betrayed him...
>**Abanazar** Indeed. A pity... Still, look on the bright side. At least he'll die wealthy... Ha ha ha ha ha ha!!!

Song 6 (Abanazar)

Audience participation

>Ah, be silent you drivelling dung-beetles. I don't have time for idle banter with imbeciles. The sands of time are running fast... (*Calling into the crack*) Hurry Aladdin, hurry! (*Aside*) You have less time than you think...

Music

Scene 9

Inside the cave. Aladdin shins down the last few feet of the rope — or appears to — and drops to the cave floor. There's a narrow shaft of daylight from overhead. Apart from that — pitch black

>**Aladdin** Well, I'm in... It's awfully dark...

Gibbering, screaming voices, accompanied by flickering ghostly lights

>You don't frighten me Spirits! I don't know the meaning of fear. Shriek all you like — you can't hurt me.

Voices and noises abate. One or two make small sounds of disappointment

>Now let me see... (*Lighting a candle*) WOW!

Low spotlight gradually comes up — piles of glittering gold and winking jewels are revealed amongst the stalagmites and stalactites

>**Abanazar** (*calling down from outside the cave*) Aladdin!
>**Aladdin** What?
>**Abanazar** Can you see the lamp?
>**Aladdin** (*to audience*) Uncle Abanazar seems mighty concerned about

his old lamp... I'm beginning to wonder about him... (*Looking around for the lamp*) ...Ah, that must be it. (*Spotting the lamp in a crevice, lifting it up and blowing the dust off it*) Huh — what a shabby old relic. Whatever can he want with it...?

Abanazar Aladdin!

Aladdin (*calling up*) Yes, all right! Keep your hair on... I've got it...

Abanazar Excellent. Bring it to me.

Aladdin It's a bit grimy... I'm just going to give it a bit of a polish...

Abanazar NO! Don't rub it whatever you do! Just bring it up to me — carefully...

Aladdin (*to himself*) This is getting more and more peculiar. There must be more to this lamp than meets the eye. (*To audience*) Do you think I should trust him?

Audience participation

No — nor do I...

Abanazar The lamp, Aladdin — hurry!

Aladdin You'll get the lamp when you get me out. But first, I'm going to help myself to a few of these jewels...

Abanazar Forget the jewels! The lamp — quickly!

Aladdin Patience, Uncle, is a virtue...

Abanazar Curse you, you insolent puppy! We don't have time to waste. Give me the lamp!

Aladdin Nobody gives me orders. You can wait a few moments until I've got what I want.

Abanazar Oh no I can't.

Aladdin Oh yes you can.

Abanazar You'll be sorry for this...

Aladdin You don't frighten me, Uncle. I don't know the meaning of fear — remember?

Abanazar You fool! You only have a few seconds left.

Aladdin What do you mean?

Abanazar The portal remains open for but seven minutes — then shuts tight for seven years!

Aladdin What?! You never told me that.

Abanazar Didn't I? Gah — silly me! Just get a wriggle on, or you'll be down there for eternity...

Aladdin I am not afraid.

Abanazar Fine — stay down there in the dark then. Perhaps you will learn the meaning of fear. Stay there and rot until doomsday!

Aladdin Uncle — no! Wait! (*He takes hold of the rope to ascend*)

Abanazar Too late! Too late, you fool!

Act I, Scene 9

The rope comes snaking down — it can be dropped from a piece of fishing line

Aladdin Uncle!!!

Graunching noise. The cave is closing

Abanazar The lamp! Lost to me! Aaaaaaaaarggggggghhhhhhhh!!!!!!
Aladdin Uncle?

The shaft of light from above goes out. It is now very dark

(*To the audience*) Drat. Now I'm trapped. I've all the riches in the world, but nowhere to spend it. And what about Jasmine? I might never see her again. What am I going to do?

Audience participation

Rub the lamp? Really? (*Gingerly, he rubs the lamp*)

There is a green flash and a puff, and The Slave of the Lamp appears. The Slave is female, bright green — and common as muck. She unfolds herself, stretching and creaking — as someone who's been bottled up in a jar for thousand years

The Slave of The Lamp Oooooooooooooooooooooooooooooooh...
Aladdin Merciful Allah — another genie!
The Slave of The Lamp Ooooh blimey — me Cilla Black's giving me gyp somefink rotten...
Aladdin I'm sorry?
The Slave of The Lamp Me back... Cooped up in there for centuries I was... (*Appearing to notice him for the first time, eyeing him up, then...*) 'Allo dearie... Been 'aving a little rub 'ave yer?
Aladdin I beg your pardon?
The Slave of The Lamp Give the old lamp a bit of a shine, did yer?
Aladdin Well, yes — but...
The Slave of The Lamp Well, that explains me sudden numinous materialisation, dunnit? I mean, it only takes a little polish and Bob's yer uncle.
Aladdin Erm, excuse me, but are you a proper genie?
The Slave of The Lamp Well I'm green aren't I?
Aladdin Yes... It's just that...
The Slave of The Lamp What?

Aladdin Well you sound a bit... you know — common.
The Slave of The Lamp Common?! Common?! Sauce! I oughta give yer a slap. Just 'cos I don' bovver wiv no airs an' graces an' all that "your wish is my command" malarkey...
Aladdin But you're supposed to hail from the mysterious East.
The Slave of The Lamp I do.
Aladdin (*doubtfully*) Really? Whereabouts?
The Slave of The Lamp Shoreditch.
Aladdin Oh for heaven's sake...
The Slave of The Lamp Look, just cos I ain't posh like you... Flamin' cheek. (*Pause*) Wotcher want anyway?
Aladdin Nothing. Unless you can help me get out of here?
The Slave of The Lamp Might.
Aladdin Pardon?
The Slave of The Lamp Might be able to help yer... If you're sure I ain't too common?
Aladdin (*becoming irritated*) What?
The Slave of The Lamp Tell you what — ask me nicely.
Aladdin (*through gritted teeth*) Please.
The Slave of The Lamp Now say it like yer mean it.
Aladdin All right — I've had enough of this... Back into the lamp...
The Slave of The Lamp (*alarmed*) What's that?
Aladdin Go on — I command you... Back into the lamp.
The Slave of The Lamp But I just bin banged up in there for a fahsand years!
Aladdin Yes, and I can see why!
The Slave of The Lamp All right — no need to go all minty on me... (*Relenting*) Oh go on then. Make a wish.
Aladdin Right, well first I want you to get me out of this rat-hole. Second, I want a big bag of gold and jewels to take with me, and thirdly, I want you to start talking like a proper genie!
The Slave of The Lamp That's three wishes that is.
Aladdin Yes? So?
The Slave of The Lamp Greedy.
Aladdin Pardon?
The Slave of The Lamp Three wishes? You'll pop.
Aladdin I'm warning you...
The Slave of The Lamp All right! All right... Keep yer hair on. (*Speaking like a genie*) Your wish is my command! Let us depart instanter!

Huge flash and Black-out!

Act I, Scene 9

Pause

The Slave of The Lamp (*a disembodied voice*) Can I talk normally now?
Aladdin (*off*) Shut up...
The Slave of The Lamp (*off*) Touchy...

Music

End of Act I

ACT II

Scene 1

Pomp and Circumstance music – Chinese-style. Lights up on the glittering throne room of Ming the Mirthless. There are huge twin thrones c, *and off to one side, a mighty hanging gong. Red and gold banners hang to either side of the stage. Lots of Oriental motifs everywhere. Grand ceremonial entrance of the assembled court. The Grand Vizier strikes his staff of office three times on the floor*

Herald All kow-tow before his Imperial Highness, Ming the Mirthless, Sultan of Ching-Chong, Ping-Pong, and Oooooagadoogoo…

Chip-Chop-Ow steps forward and swings a donger to connect with the giant gong. Unfortunately he gets the sound effect of a three inch dinner gong! He regards his donger in mild consternation. The smallest available attendant — a child — now steps forward, shakes his head in disgust at the executioner's evident ineptitude, wrests the donger from Chip-Chop-Ow, twirls it with pancache, and then slugs the gong. Sound effect of a huge reverberating dong

> *The small attendant thrusts the donger back into the hands of the glaring Chip-Chop-Ow and nonchalantly saunters off*

> *More music, and the Sultan and Sultana enter to take their places upon the twin thrones. Princess Jasmine enters behind them attended by Pee-Long. They take their places to one side. There is much murmuring amongst the courtiers and servants. During the following, an attendant places a tray of savouries in front of Ming, and a messenger runs on, hands a card to the Grand Vizier, kow-tows, and runs off again*

The Grand Vizier Utter silence for his Imperial Highness, Ming the Mirthless, Sultan of Ching-Chong, Ping-Pong, and Oooooagadoogoo!
Ming the Mirthless (*meekly*) Hallo everybody… What's occurring?
No-Lo-Fat (*shortly*) Executions. First up — that horrid little peasant that ogled our beloved yum-yum doughnut.

Act II, Scene 1

Princess Jasmine Mother — please! I'm not a china doll to be mollycoddled. I don't care who looks at me.
No-Lo-Fat It's got nothing to do with you. If the lower orders get the idea they can raise their eyes to their betters, it won't be long before they start raising their hands against us too. No, the wretch is going to be parted from his insolent head, and that's that.
Princess Jasmine (*appealing to Ming the Mirthless*) Daddy, say something, please!
Ming the Mirthless (*looking up from where he has been perusing the savouries*) Erm... Anyone for a crispy won-ton?

The Grand Vizier coughs politely

No-Lo-Fat What is it?
The Grand Vizier Highness, there is a visitor below. (*Reading from the card*) His Most Royal Excellency, Prince Wai-No-Dong of the city of Sum-Tin-Wong wishes to present his credentials...
No-Lo-Fat Does he indeed? Never heard of him.
The Grand Vizier Further, he begs leave to solicit your approval for a match between his royal personage and Her Most Fragrant Delectableness, the Princess Jasmine.
Princess Jasmine NO!
No-Lo-Fat Quite right. Absolutely not. The impertinence of it.
The Grand Vizier (*waving forward another attendant who places an ornately-carved mahogany chest on the floor before the Sultan and Sultana*) Further, he sends this trifling token of his esteem for the all-powerful Sultanate of Ching-Chong, Ping-Pong, and Oooooagadoogoo... (*He gestures*)

The attendant opens the chest to reveal piles of gold coins and jewels

Ming the Mirthless Good grief! Look at all that wonga. And all those precious stones. (*Stooping to rummage in the box*) And... I say... a Spice Girls CD. Truly, this is a gift fit for an Emperor...
No-Lo-Fat Very well. Send him up.
The Grand Vizier (*appalled*) Oh I couldn't possibly.
No-Lo-Fat Just show him in, you idiot.
The Grand Vizier (*bowing out*) Yes, Highness.
No-Lo-Fat Well husband, perhaps we've finally found a suitor to take our wayward child in hand...
Princess Jasmine I'll never marry him — never! I don't care how rich he is. My heart belongs to Aladdin.
No-Lo-Fat Well in that case, while we're waiting, we'll dispose of the

prisoners, shall we? (*She claps her hands*)

An attendant runs off

Princess Jasmine Mother, no! If you harm one hair of Aladdin's head, I'll never speak to you again.
No-Lo-Fat Oh do be quiet, you silly girl. I can't believe you're getting into such a tizz about topping a couple of peasants. These people die like flies all the time. They're not like us you know.

Hoo-Poo and Hee-Pong enter, ushering in Sinbad and Widow Twankee

Hoo-Poo (*announcing*) The prisoners, Aladdin and Widow Twankee.
Princess Jasmine (*can't bear to watch, turning away with a stifled cry*) Aladdin...
No-Lo-Fat Well, no point beating about the bush. You're both for the chop. Any last words?
Widow Twankee Yes. You smell.
No-Lo-Fat Fine. Nose-chop first, then your head. (*To Sinbad*) You?
Sinbad Can I tell you about my seven incredible voyages?
No-Lo-Fat Sorry — we don't have three weeks to spare. Busy day — you know how it is.
Princess Jasmine (*burying her head in Pee-Long's shoulder and sobbing*) Oh Aladdin...
Pee-Long (*doing the same*) Oh Aladdin...
Princess Jasmine (*looking up; surprised*) What do you mean "Oh Aladdin"?
Pee-Long I love him...
Princess Jasmine No you don't! I love him.
Pee-Long Then we both love him.

Weeping with renewed grief, they bury their heads in each others shoulders

Widow Twankee Oi! I love him too you know... That reminds me — I wonder where he's got to....
No-Lo-Fat Who?
Widow Twankee Aladdin.
Princess Jasmine Aladdin? Why he's standing right there. (*Seeing Sinbad properly for the first time*) Wait a minute — that's not Aladdin!
Pee-Long Oh yes it is.

Act II, Scene 1

Princess Jasmine Oh no it isn't.
No-Lo-Fat Oh yes it is.
Widow Twankee Oh no it isn't.
Hoo-Poo Oh yes it is.
Sinbad Oh no it isn't.
Ming the Mirthless Oh do give it a rest, the lot of you. (*To Sinbad*) If you're not Aladdin, who are you?
Sinbad I am Sinbad the Sailor.
Ming the Mirthless (*crossly*) Well what the bloody hell are you doing in "Aladdin" then?!
Sinbad It's a long story…
Widow Twankee (*to the audience*) Like all his stories…
No-Lo-Fat Well if you're Sinbad — where's Aladdin?
Widow Twankee Now that, is a very good question.
No-Lo-Fat Right — off with her head.
Widow Twankee Or maybe not such a good question…

The Grand Vizier enters

The Grand Vizier (*announcing*) His Most Royal Excellency, Prince Wai-No-Dong.
No-Lo-Fat Never mind that. Grand Vizier — where is Aladdin?
The Grand Vizier (*taken by surprise*) Aladdin? Why he's er… He's…

Aladdin strides on, now gorgeously dressed in fine princely attire

Aladdin Here.
The Grand Vizier Wai-No-Dong!
Aladdin (*aside to the Grand Vizier on his way past*) I'll tell you later…
Princess Jasmine Aladdin!
Widow Twankee Aladdin!
No-Lo-Fat Aladdin? (*To Hoo-Poo and Hee-Pong*) Seize him!
Aladdin (*holding up a hand to forestall them*) Why would you do that?
No-Lo-Fat Because you, a common coolie, only dared to lay your worthless eyes upon my precious daughter!
Aladdin Excuse me, but I didn't only dare to lay eyes on her…
No-Lo-Fat No?
Aladdin No. (*Pause*) I laid hands on her too.
No-Lo-Fat Hands?!!!
Aladdin Yes. Just before I kissed her.
No-Lo-Fat Kissed her?!!!

Pandemonium breaks out

(*Swooning*) Head-chop, this instant!

Chip-Chop-Ow steps forward and unshoulders his chopper

Aladdin But I am no common coolie. I'm a Prince. In fact, I'm the wealthiest Prince in all China.
No-Lo-Fat (*recovering*) You are?
Aladdin I am.
Widow Twankee (*amazed*) You are?
Aladdin I am.
Widow Twankee (*aside*) Uncle Abanazar came through then?
Aladdin (*aside*) You could say that... (*To the court*) I own three principalities and a palace wrought from marble and gold. It has a thousand rooms and two dozen minarets capped in lapis lazuli. The corridors are paved with emeralds, whilst the gardens and pools are the most fragrant and beautiful this side of Paradise.
All Cooo...
Aladdin Grant me your daughter's hand in marriage, and she will want for nothing. For neither food nor drink, warmth nor comfort. (*Turning to Princess Jasmine*) Jasmine — do you love me?
Princess Jasmine Oh, Aladdin, yes!
Aladdin (*turning back to Ming the Mirthless*) Then least of all, will she want for love.
Ming the Mirthless Well, it's a yes from me. I couldn't be more delighted — unless I was going to live there myself obviously. (*Sotto voce to Aladdin; with a sideways glancing at No-Lo-Fat*) I don't suppose..?
No-Lo-Fat Foolish man. This boy has a silver tongue, not a golden palace. How did he acquire these sudden riches? How become a Prince, when but yesterday he was a pauper? This is all some trumpery...
Aladdin I cannot blame you for doubting me. The transformation in my fortunes has been sudden indeed. But fortune, they say, favours the brave — and I do not know fear. Unless it be the fear of living without the one I love.
No-Lo-Fat Oh please, you're making me nauseous...
Aladdin To prove my worth, I have brought you other gifts. (*He claps his hands*)

An attendant brings on another box

Act II, Scene 1

(*Opening and presenting to Ming the Mirthless*) For you, Mighty Sultan — father-of-my-bride-to-be — a forty-Gig Sony Playstation Three with a full set of shoot-'em-up games and the latest version of Grand Theft Auto Four.
Ming the Mirthless Oh I say, my boy! That's awfully decent of you... (*He starts inspecting his toys*)
Aladdin And for you, my Sultana, a most rare and special gift... From the bamboo forests high in the mountains of Sichuan, I bring you a new playmate and most endearing pet.
No-Lo-Fat (*sourly*) If it's a tarantula, I've already got one.
Aladdin Much better than that... (*He claps his hands*)

An attendant leads on Noo-Noo the pantomime panda... The court reacts in astonishment

All Ooooooh...
Aladdin This exquisite animal is known as panda. She is called Noo-Noo — a pet fit for an Empress...
No-Lo-Fat (*impressed despite herself*) Well she is rather pretty. She'd make a lovely coat...
Princess Jasmine Mother!
No-Lo-Fat Just thinking aloud... (*To Aladdin*) Well, you seem to have established your bonafides young man. I suppose we must not look a gift horse in the mouth. You may wed our daughter. What do you say, O husband?
Ming the Mirthless What? Eh? Oh yes... yes, of course... (*To Aladdin*) Tell me, is this backwards-compatible with a Sinclair Spectrum?
Princess Jasmine Oh Aladdin!

They run to embrace

No-Lo-Fat Stop that at once! There are preparations to be made. Tonight, Jasmine will travel to your palace in Sum-Tin-Wong. There she will spend the night in lone contemplation, making ready for her wedding day. Tomorrow, there will be a royal progress. You will join us. The dowry will be one hundred million billion trillion nik-niks...
Aladdin Not a problem.
Widow Twankee (*aside; aghast*) But that's nearly a fiver!
Aladdin (*aside*) Mum — I know what I'm doing...
No-Lo-Fat Now kindly take your wretched mother and get out of our sight. Tomorrow midday, we meet outside the city gates and journey in a procession of a hundred emasculated elephants to the golden towers of Sum-Tin-Wong, where your bride will be waiting for you,

serene, fragrant and delectable. (*To Princess Jasmine*) You — go to your chambers and prepare. You have a long road ahead of you, my daughter.
Aladdin (*to Princess Jasmine*) Well then. Until tomorrow…
Princess Jasmine Tomorrow…

They hold hands and kiss fleetingly

No-Lo-Fat All right. Enough. Everybody out! I am retiring to play with my Noo-Noo.
Widow Twankee (*aside*) Well, there's a first time for everything…
Sinbad What about me?
No-Lo-Fat You can get out too. One Aladdin is quite enough. Two would be intolerable. But be warned, imposter. Leave the city by nightfall. If you are found in Peking come the dawn, your head will be forfeit!

She sweeps off

Everyone looks at each other

The Lights fade

Scene 2

A clearing

Lights come up to a spooky greeny-blue. A sinister gong sounds, and Mrs Cheng enters

   Song 7 (Mrs Cheng, accompanied by a pair of pirate dancers)

After the song

Mrs Cheng An entire day in this teeming antheap, and still Sinbad eludes me. How I long for the open sea, the roll of a deck beneath my feet, and the thunder of the guns.

The rest of the pirates rush onstage in a mob

Nip-Tuk Mrs Cheng! Mrs Cheng!
Mrs Cheng What?
Kung Po Prawn We found somefink…

Act II, Scene 2   49

Mrs Cheng What?
Wong-Ki-I This.

They push forward Hoo-Poo and Hee-Pong, disarmed and dishevelled

Hoo-Poo Get off us, foul-smelling boat people!

The pirates cluster around them, poking them with their knives and pistols

Mrs Cheng Ah. These look suspiciously like police persons.
Hee-Pong Too right we are. And you under arrest, see?

Wong-Ki-I hits Hee-Pong in the face with his foam rubber cudgel. Biff

Hee-Pong See?

Biff

Hee-Pong See?

Biff. Wong-Ki-I gets ready to biff him again, but Hee-Pong just glares mutely at him

Mrs Cheng Finished?

Hee-Pong nods sullenly

> Good... It seems you are mistaken... You are the ones under arrest. Which is just as well — for you. Because if I thought you were police persons, it would be my solemn duty as a pirate to cut you into a thousand little pieces, and feed you to my pet crocodiles.

Hoo-Poo Oh no, we're definitely not police persons.
Mrs Cheng (*musing*) And yet, you are dressed as police persons...
Hoo-Poo We just on way to fancy dress party.
Hee-Pong That right. In fac' we are... er... (*improvising*) ...children's entertainers.
Mrs Cheng Oh really?
Hoo-Poo Yeah. (*Glaring at Hee-Pong*) Really.
Mrs Cheng Very well, go ahead — entertain these children.
Hoo-Poo I'm sorry?
Mrs Cheng (*gesturing to the audience*) These children — make them laugh.   ?
Hoo-Poo Laugh?

Mrs Cheng Yes, laugh. Entertain them — you live. If not — crispy balls.
Hoo-Poo (*swallowing hard*) Ulp.
Wong-Ki-I (*leering*) No pressure.

Mrs Cheng moves DL. *The rest of the pirates all move to sit chattering and excited on the floor stage* R, *like a lot of expectant children at a party... The following round of quickfire Chinese gags is played partly to the actual children in the audience, and partly to the pirate audience seated on stage*

Hoo-Poo (*nervously*) All right then... Well, er... Hallo kiddies... Would you like to hear a joke? I say, I say, I say... Why did the chicken cross the road?

Audience participation... ("To get to the other side" or "to see his flatmate" or whatever...)

No. Because he didn't like the flyover... Fly over, get it?

The pirates don't think much of this. They mumble threateningly amongst themselves

Hee-Pong (*regarding them dubiously*) Hoo-Poo, I don't think that right punchline.
Hoo-Poo Shut your face. Hey — I know. What you shout to get served in Chinese warehouse?
Hee-Pong I give up.
Hoo-Poo Supplies! (*Surprise*)

The pirates laugh uproariously

Hee-Pong ...All right then, what you call a Chinese woman with one leg?

Hoo-Poo shrugs — he doesn't know

Irene. (*He leans over comically on one leg to illustrate the point, then falls over*)

The pirates roar with laughter and slap their thighs in appreciation. And so it goes on through the following jokes

Act II, Scene 2

Hoo-Poo All right then — why do all Chinese tourists visit Harrow?
Hee-Pong I don't know, why do all Chinese tourists visit Harrow?
Hoo-Poo Because when they catch taxi at Heathrow Airport, they say (*waving*): "harro mister taxi driver..." Hey — why should you never use the telephone directory in Peking?
Hee-Pong I don't know, why should you never use the telephone directory in Peking?
Hoo-Poo Because half the people are Wings and the other half are Wongs.
Hee-Pong So?
Hoo-Poo So if you not velly careful, you might wing the wong number.
Hee-Pong That was rubbish. Shall I do my Bangkok joke?
Hoo-Poo Hmmm... (*Looking doubtfully at the onstage audience*) ... Maybe not.
Hee-Pong It's going well — keep it up...
Hoo-Poo All right — I went into Chinese restaurant and say to waiter "Do you do take away?" He say, "sure — I do takeaway — seven from ten leaves three".
Hee-Pong All right — What is Bruce Lee's favourite drink? WWWAAAATTTAAAHHH!!!
Hoo-Poo What you call Chinese woman with food mixer on head? Blenda.
Hee-Pong What time is it when Chinaman go to dentist? Two fifteen! Hahahahahahaha. Two fifteen, geddit?

The pirates look at each other in incomprehension

Hoo-Poo Two thirty.
Hee-Pong Oh yah — tooth-hurty. I 'member...

The pirates now begin to mutter mutinously amongst themselves again. They are not impressed

Hoo-Poo Quick, we're losing them. Do something funny.
Hee-Pong What?
Hoo-Poo Hit me.
Hee-Pong I'm sorry?
Hoo-Poo (*shouting*) HIT ME!

Hee-Pong obliges — bonk. The pirates laugh

Again.

Bonk. The pirates laugh more

Again! Again!

Hee-Pong hits him — Bonk. Bonk. Bonk. Bonk. Bonk. Hoo-Poo falls to the floor. The pirates laugh uproariously

Mrs Cheng Enough! I am convinced. You are indeed children's entertainers. You are far too stupid to be policemen.
Hee-Pong (*aside*) You obviously haven't met many policemen... (*He delivers a sly kick to Hoo-Poo to illustrate the point*)
Hoo-Poo (*getting up with difficulty*) Excellent. Then we'll be on our way.
Hee-Pong Chin-chin.
Hoo-Poo Toodle-oo.
Hee-Pong Pip-Pip.
Hoo-Poo And Na-Poo.

As one they bow and head for the exit. Mrs Cheng clicks her devilish curly fingernails, and as one, her pirate gang spring to their feet, bristling with weapons

Mrs Cheng Wait!

Swallowing with fear, Hoo-Poo and Hee-Pong turn back

I am looking for someone. Someone special...
Hoo-Poo (*aside to Hee-Pong*) I'm not surprised.
Mrs Cheng Sinbad the Sailor. Have you seen him?
Hoo-Poo } (*together*) { Yes.
Hee-Pong } { No.

They exchange glances, then...

Hoo-Poo } (*together*) { No.
Hee-Pong } { Yes.

They exchange glances again. They have been rumbled...

Hoo-Poo (*reluctantly*) Sinbad been banished from the city. Must be gone before dawn tomorrow.
Mrs Cheng Excellent. Then all we need to do is watch the City gates, and we will have him. Anything else?

Act II, Scene 2   53

Hoo-Poo (*to Hee-Pong*) Should we tell them?
Hee-Pong Hoo-Poo, I don't think we should talk.
Hoo-Poo Fine. We'll just let them kill us shall we?
Hee-Pong On second thoughts, let's spill the beans.
Hoo-Poo Very well. (*To Mrs Cheng*) Sinbad go with Aladdin.
Hee-Pong And Aladdin live at Happy Tub Laundry.
Hoo-Poo There is secret gate in city wall not far from Happy Tub Laundry.
Hee-Pong So that the way they will go.
Hoo-Poo Simple process of deduction.
Hee-Pong NOT that we are police persons... (*He says, flexing his knees like a comedy policeman*)
Hoo-Poo No indeed. (*He too flexes his knees like a comedy policeman. Then salutes*)
Mrs Cheng Excellent. (*To pirates*) You know what to do.
Pirates (*in unison*) Yes, Mrs Cheng.
Mrs Cheng Better not screw-up this time.
Pirates (*in unison*) No, Mrs Cheng.
Mrs Cheng Or no pocket moncy!
Pirates (*in unison*) No pocket money!

Mrs Cheng sweeps imperiously off

Hoo-Poo turns hopefully to Wong-Ki-I and Nip-Tuk

Hoo-Poo Ah so... Now you let us go, yes?
Nip-Tuk No. Now you come with us — show hidden gate... (*To the rest of the pirates*) Bring them.
Hee-Pong Nooooo!

Hoo-Poo and Hee-Pong are engulfed and roughly bundled offstage by the pirates

The Lights fade

Scene 3

Interior. The Twankees' laundry. The table and chairs are there, UR — with the lamp sitting on the kitchen table. One of the washing lines is still up, but the washing has now changed to a different array of comical laundry items, which Widow Twankee is just finishing pinning on the line, from a basket held by Wishee-Washee. There is a knock at the door. Widow Twankee crosses to open the door. A small child steps in bearing a folded slip of paper

Messenger Message for Wankee…
Widow Twankee Twankee.
Messenger Oh yeah — velly solly.
Widow Twankee You will be. Hand it over.

The messenger does so

Now beat it.

The messenger bows and exits

Wishee-Washee (*coming across to peer at the note*) What that?
Widow Twankee Oh, it's from my dressmaker. He's ready for me second fitting… (*Coming down to the audience*) I'm having a posh frock made for the wedding, ladies… Finest organza, taffeta, hessian and lycra. Oh yus, well, we can afford the best now y'know. No more slummin' it for me. I'm quality now, I am. Right — Wishee-Washee, you stay here. An' whatever you do, don't let that funny old lamp out of your sight, right?
Wishee-Washee Light.
Widow Twankee No, it's a lamp, right?
Wishee-Washee Light.
Widow Twankee Oh, I give up. I don't know what's so special about it, but Aladdin was most insistent that we keep it safe and sound.
Wishee-Washee Hey, where Aladdin go?
Widow Twankee To show Sinbad where to slip out of the city unnoticed. Mrs Cheng's gangsters are skulking on every corner, all looking out for him. So you watch out while I'm gone — and remember, never open the door to strangers.
Wishee-Washee Hokai! I 'member.
Widow Twankee Spiffin'. See you later then.

Widow Twankee exits

Act II, Scene 3

Wishee-Washee starts to sweep up, whistling to himself... Then after two or three seconds

Abanazar (*off*) New lamps for old!
Wishee-Washee Now what?
Abanazar (*off, closer*) New lamps for old!

There is a hammering on the door... Wishee-Washee opens it and shouts

Wishee-Washee Hey! You push off. Wishee-Washee no go talkee strange men...

Abanazar pushes past him into the room. He is disguised as an old gypsy pedlar. He has a gnarly stick over his shoulder with an array of lamps suspended from it

Abanazar New lamps for old! (*Squinting at Wishee-Washee*) Greetings young master. I am an itinerant street vendor.
Wishee-Washee No thanks. We already got one.
Abanazar (*taken aback*) Eh? One what?
Wishee-Washee A street.
Abanazar What?
Wishee-Washee You street vendor, yah? You selling streets?
Abanazar No, I am selling lamps. Or to be precise, I'm giving them away. Providing you have an old one to exchange that is...
Wishee-Washee But we don' have no lamps.
Abanazar That, my boy, is a double negative, which means you most certainly do... (*Spotting the magic lamp standing on a table*) And, oh look — there it is...
Wishee-Washee (*suspiciously*) Why you give shiny new lamp for crummy old one?
Abanazar Ah — recycling — carbon offsetting — it's all the rage. Haven't you heard?
Wishee-Washee No...
Abanazar Well, it's like this: You give me an old lamp. I give you a lovely shiny new one. End of. It's all about renewable energy.
Wishee-Washee Well. I dunno... Aladdin velly fond of his old lamp. He say take special care of it.
Abanazar Perhaps if I were just to take a look at it... That couldn't hurt could it?
Wishee-Washee Well — hokai, but it pretty ropey. (*He fetches the magic lamp, returns with it and shows it to Abanazar*)

Abanazar   Ah yes, very tarnished... Very old... It can't work properly...
Wishee-Washee   Yeah, you probabry light. Here... (*He offers the lamp*)

Music builds — then, just as Abanazar is about to take it in his eagerly twitching fingers, Wishee-Washee changes his mind and whisks it away from him

No. Not fair. Can't ask shiny new lamp for this old fing.
Abanazar (*desperately*) Yes you can.
Wishee-Washee   No. Can't.
Abanazar (*more desperately*) You can! You can!
Wishee-Washee (*dubiously*) Well, if you sure...
Abanazar   Oh I'm sure...

Once again Wishee-Washee is about to hand over the lamp. Once more the music starts to build. Then he changes his mind again

Wishee-Washee   Wait. (*To audience*) What you fink? Should we swap old lamp for shiny new one?

Audience participation

No. I fink we keep old one.
Abanazar (*starting to lose his cool*) Give it to me...
Wishee-Washee   No, I don' fink so.
Abanazar (*threateningly*) Give it to me...
Wishee-Washee (*backing away*) Now don' you go all hot 'n' sour on me...
Abanazar (*containing himself with difficulty*) Give it to me, and I'll not only give you this gleaming new lamp in its place, I'll give you fifty golden dinars into the bargain.
Wishee-Washee   Wow! Recycling mus' be velly important.
Abanazar (*fervently*) Oh believe me, it is.
Wishee-Washee   Fine. Take it.

He plonks the lamp into Abanazar's grasp. The magician visibly shudders as he finally gets his hands on the coveted artefact...

Abanazar (*softly*) Thank you, Wishee-Washee.
Wishee-Washee   Pleasure... (*Pause*) Wishee-Washee? Hey — how you know my name? I no say...

Act II, Scene 3

Abanazar pulls off his disguise and Wishee-Washee recognizes him at once

YOU!!!
Abanazar Yes — me! And now you will see my true colours, and they are black, black, black! Ha ha ha ha ha!!!
Wishee-Washee (*to audience*) Uh-oh…

Abanazar caresses the lamp — and in his hands it is an obscene motion

Abanazar (*intoning*) O Slave of The Lamp — I Summon Thee! Hocus-Pocus, Sim-Sala-Bim, Alakazam!

Brief Black-out. Green flash

The Slave of The Lamp materialises

Ha ha ha ha ha ha ha!!!!
The Slave of The Lamp 'Allo sailor.
Abanazar (*gloating horribly*) At last! The lamp is mine! Unbridled power is mine! Ha ha ha ha ha ha!!!

Audience participation

The Slave of The Lamp Hold on, you're not Aladdin.
Abanazar No. I'm not. Aladdin is finished. You're my slave now — and I have work for you.
The Slave of The Lamp Work? I don't like the sound of that…
Abanazar First, to Sum-Tin-Wong, to the golden palace you created for that gobby little upstart, Aladdin. I am going to take everything he has. His palace, his princess — and his precious pluck. He was nothing when I found him, and when I've finished with him, he'll be less than nothing. Whilst I shall be rolling in gold, girls and glory! His gold! His girl! And his glory! Oh it's all too delicious! Ha ha ha ha ha! Come slave — away. Let's ride!
The Slave of The Lamp Your wish is my command. I s'pose…

Brief Black-out. Flash

Abanazar and The Slave of The Lamp both vanish

Wishee-Washee (*to audience*) Oh dear. Wishee-Washee in deep plop.

Better go find Aladdin. Break bad news...

He trots off

The Lights fade

Scene 4

A street. Widow Twankee enters, munching her way through a huge bag of sweets... If necessary this scene can start in front of the main tabs to allow time for the laundry to be cleared

Widow Twankee (*to audience*) Ooooh, I've just had me second fitting, ladies and gentlemen. And guess what? There was a bit of slack around me gusset! Yes, so I'm having to eat this big bag of sweeties to make sure I fill out me frock properly. Oh — I'm going to be the Belle of the Ball! Who'd have thought it, my good-for-nothing son marrying into royalty... Oh and I shall ride an elephant. Oooh I do love animals, don't you, boys and girls? Yes...

At this point, the main tabs open on to a more or less bare stage — or with a street scene — and Noo-Noo the panda wanders on behind Widow Twankee

Audience participation

What's behind me?

"It's behind you" routine, with Widow Twankee looking first one way, then the other, accusing the audience of being a rotten bunch of fibbers and so on. Eventually, Noo-Noo sidles up from behind and taps Widow Twankee on the shoulder

Excuse me! What are you doing here? You're supposed to be keeping the Sultana amused.

Noo-Noo shakes her head vehemently

You don't like the Sultana?

Noo-Noo shakes her head

No, well, can't say I blame you...

Act II, Scene 4

Noo-Noo beckons. Widow Twankee leans down and Noo-Noo whispers in her ear

She's going to make you into a fur coat? Of course she's not... (*To the audience*) she wouldn't do a thing like that — would she boys and girls?

Audience participation. Noo-Noo looks alarmed and whispers in Widow Twankee's ear again

Can you come home with me? Certainly not...

Noo-Noo looks sad and elicits an...

Audience Aaaaaaaaaaaaaaaaaah...
Widow Twankee Oh don't pander to it ladies and gentlemen... (*Boom Boom*) ...Panda to it — geddit?! D'you see what I did then? "Panda to it..." These are the jokes, folks! (*Pause*) Oh forget it...

Noo-Noo whispers in Widow Twankee's ear again

Can you have my bag of sweeties? No you jolly well can't — cheek! I shall waste away if I don't keep me strength up...

Noo-Noo looks behind Widow Twankee and casts a disbelieving glance at her enormous posterior

(*Catching the look and glaring at Noo-Noo*) 'Ere, I know. I shall return you to the wild... How about that?

Noo-Noo shrugs disconsolately

(*Regarding Noo-Noo with a bit more sympathy*) Dear me. You are down in the dumps, aren't you? ...I know — How about a song?

Noo-Noo claps

Oh, you like singing? Excellent. What's your favourite song then?

Noo-Noo whispers

"*Two Lovely Black Eyes*"? ...I'm not sure anyone here is old enough to remember that one, dear...

Noo-Noo whispers again

"*The Old Bamboo*"? No, I'm sorry, but I'm not doing *Dick Van Dyke* for all the tea in China... What about "*My Aunt Came Back From Old Peking*"

Noo-Noo shrugs. She doesn't know it

...Ooooh. I know... We can get some of these boys and girls to come up and join in. What do you think of that?

Noo-Noo claps again

Right then... (*To the children in the audience*) Who'd like to come up and sing a little song to put a smile on my little furry Noo-Noo? Anyone who comes up gets some of my yummy sweeties...

Song 8 (Audience participation number...)

*This is a variant of the old campfire song "*My Aunt Came Back From (Wherever)*"*

It's a call and repeat song whereby Widow Twankee sings a line, the chorus repeat it, and so on The fun however, comes from the fact that each verse has an action. The actions build, so that at the end of the first verse the chorus are doing one action, by the end of the second verse they're doing two actions together, by the end of the third verse, three actions — and so on. It's rather like the old rubbing your tummy whilst patting yourself on the head challenge

This needs careful explanation by Widow Twankee, and a practice run with the first verse and action. Noo-Noo should be positioned out front and used to demonstrate the different actions. Other members of the company can be brought onstage costumed as citizens to assist as required

My aunt came back

Chorus repeat: My aunt came back

From Singapore

Repeat: From Singapore

Act II, Scene 4   61

And she brought with her

Repeat: And she brought with her

A carnivore

Repeat: A carnivore

Action 1: miming a scary tiger's paw with the right hand

My aunt came back
From Old Kowloon
And she brought with her
A wooden spoon

Add action 2: stirring a pot with the left hand

My aunt came back
From Old Peking
And she brought with her
A bouncy spring

Add action 3: hopping up and down on the right leg

My aunt came back
From Nanky-Poo
And she brought with her
A wooden shoe

Add action 4: stamping left foot on the floor between hops

My aunt came back
From Shanghai fair
And she brought with her
A rocking chair

Add action 5: rocking to and fro like a crazed asylum inmate — whilst clawing, stirring, hopping and stomping!

This can of course be continued ad infinitum by adding more verses and actions, but five verses are usually enough

The song is followed by rounds of applause, distribution of sweets —

Widow Twankee takes a big fat toffee for herself — and the audience participants being helped back down the stairs into the auditorium

After all of which, Noo-Noo manages to slope off with what remains of the bag of sweets

(*Regaining the stage*) Oh, that was pandemonium ladies and gentlemen. "Panda-monium" geddit?! Oh yes — I'm here all week, folks! (*Pause*; *chewing*) ...and so's this sweet! Note to self — avoid the toffees in future... (*Looking around*) Hang on a minute... Where's that perishin' panda gone? And where's my bag of sweeties?! Oooh, the rotten thieving furball. I dunno about bamboo — I've been bamboozled! Pesky thing...

Wishee-Washee runs on

Wishee-Washee Widow Twankee, Widow Twankee!
Widow Twankee Wishee-Washee, what's the matter?
Wishee-Washee We been robbed. Nuncle Nabanazar come back — steal lamp.
Widow Twankee Oh Gawd. That's not good... Right, let's find Aladdin and break the bad news. You go that way, I'll go this way.

They each attempt to exit the opposite ways to where she has just pointed, promptly bump into each other, right themselves, and both go off in the wrong direction

The Lights fade

SCENE 5

The lighting state changes somewhat, but the minimal street scene remains unchanged. The stage needs to be largely clear for the dance routine that follows in this scene. Aladdin and Sinbad enter L

Aladdin Well, the back gate to the city is just over there... You should be safe now. A short walk down to the Yellow River, and you can pick up a ship to the coast, and thence for the Indies. I'm sorry you've got to go, Sinbad, but this panto ain't big enough for the both of us.
Sinbad I quite understand. I wouldn't be too chuffed if you showed up in my panto either.

Suddenly the Chinese pirates burst on R

Act II, Scene 5   63

Nip-Tuk Hold it right there, ladyboys!
Sinbad Uh-oh.
Wong-Ki-I Which one of you two pansies is Sinbad?
Sinbad (*stepping forward*) I'm Sinbad.

A short pause

Aladdin (*stepping forward*) No — I'm Sinbad.
Sinbad Aladdin, what are you doing?
Wong-Wei (*stepping forward inappropriately*) I'm Sinbad! And so my brother.
Kung Po Prawn (*patiently*) No, you are Wong-Wei. And your brother is Wun-Wei.
Wong-Wei Ah so. My bad. Solly. (*He steps back into line*)
Nip-Tuk Two Sinbads — well, well… An embarrassment of lychees. We just have to kill you both.
Aladdin You can try.
Wong-Ki-I You have something that belongs to my mistress…
Sinbad Mrs Cheng!
Wong-Ki-I Do not speak her name aloud, mongrel.
Sinbad Mrs Cheng!
Wong-Ki-I I tol' you not to do that.
Nip-Tuk We make you offer. Return what you stole from her, and we kill you quickly.
Kung Po Prawn If not, we kill you slowly, then take it anyway.

All the pirates laugh exaggeratedly

Sinbad I stole nothing.
Wong-Ki-I You lie.
Aladdin No, you lie, vermin.
Sinbad It's all right Aladdin — this isn't your fight. Walk away while you still can.
Aladdin Walk away? (*Considering for a moment, then…*) I don't know what that means.
Sinbad But you're getting married tomorrow… To the girl of your dreams.
Aladdin That's true… We'd better make this quick then.
Sinbad Oh, it'll be quick — I'm a black belt.
Aladdin Me too.
Sinbad Excellent… Taekwondo or jujitsu?
Aladdin (*narrowly*) Feng Shui.
Sinbad Better leave this to me.

Aladdin No chance.

Music. All spring into extreme martial arts postures

Nip-Tuk Shall we?
Sinbad Let's.

Kung-Fu instrumental as Aladdin, Sinbad and the pirates engage in an elaborate spoof martial arts dance routine, preferably with some "flying" along rooflines in the manner of art house martial arts movies... By the end of the fight, the pirates are all laid out or have scarpered, leaving Sinbad and Aladdin to dust their hands

Aladdin Well, that's put them straight...
Sinbad They'll be back... Thank you my friend. I am sorry I brought this trouble upon you. The sooner I quit Peking, the better for all of us.

Wishee-Washee enters

Wishee-Washee Aladdin! Aladdin!
Aladdin Wishee-Washee... What's wrong?
Wishee-Washee Nuncle Nabanazar — he come back.... Take lamp.
Aladdin He took the lamp? How?
Wishee-Washee Big magic. And that not all. Your palace — it vanished.
Aladdin My palace? But Jasmine was at my palace!
Wishee-Washee Yeah — she vanish too. Thin air. Poof.
Aladdin Abanazar! He has stolen Jasmine.

Pee-Long runs on

Pee-Long Aladdin! There you are. I've been looking everywhere for you.
Aladdin Now what?
Pee-Long The Sultana has ordered your arrest.
Aladdin Me? Why?
Pee-Long She says you deceived the Sultan. Your palace and riches were all an illusion, and now they've vanished and her daughter with them. She's hopping mad. You'd best make yourself scarce.
Aladdin What am I going to do? How am I ever going to find Jasmine?
Sinbad We'll search for her. We'll sail the seven seas and scour the

Act II, Scene 5

corners of the earth until we find her.

Aladdin (*despondently*) We'll never find her. Abanazar wields the lamp. Its magic is immense. It will take magic to find him.

Sinbad In that case, I might have something that will help.

Aladdin What?

Sinbad A curiosity. I acquired it on my seventh and final voyage... Would you like to hear about it?

Aladdin (*doubtfully*) Do we have time?

Sinbad Possibly not. (*Pulling out a small pouch*) In truth, I took it from someone... She wasn't very happy about it...

Aladdin Mrs Cheng...

Sinbad Yes. Though she had stolen it from its rightful owner, I won it off her fair and square...

Aladdin Poker?

Sinbad Top Trumps.

Aladdin (*impressed*) Wow. What is it?

Sinbad A ring.

Aladdin She pursued you halfway round the world just for an old ring?

Sinbad It's not "just a ring" Aladdin. It is potent magic. If you can master its power, you could use it to find Jasmine.

Aladdin But it's not mine to command. The ring belongs to you.

Sinbad No. (*Pressing the ring into Aladdin's hand*) It's yours.

Aladdin (*incredulous*) Don't you want it?

Sinbad Of course — I've risked my life to possess it. But your need is the greater.

Pee-Long Oh Sinbad. My hero...

Aladdin Thank you my friend. (*Looking closely at the ring*) Wait a minute... I've seen one of these before. It's a Ying and Yang ring.

Sinbad It's what?

Wishee-Washee Ying and Yang. The forces of darkness and light... The antitheses or mutual correlations in human perceptions of dynamic phenomena in the natural world, combining to create a unity of opposites...

Sinbad Blimey!

Wishee-Washee (*aside*) Wikipedia.

Sinbad (*aside*) Oh, right...

Aladdin My Uncle Abanazar had the Ying, this is the Yang... Is this what I think it is?

Sinbad I don't know. I've never risked using it.

Aladdin Well, let's give it a go shall we...

Wishee-Washee Aladdin — no!

Aladdin rubs the ring. There is a split-second Black-out and a mighty flash-bang

> *The Slave of The Ring stands before them. But this Slave of The Ring appears much bigger and more powerful than before*

Sinbad Wow!
The Slave of The Ring (*in a huge, booming voice*) HO HO HO HO! COWER O YE PUNY MORTALS! LOOK ON MY WORKS AND DESPAIR!

> *Pause. Aladdin, Sinbad, Wishee-Washee and Pee-Long stare at him. The Slave of The Ring gradually seems to dwindle. He looks a bit shamefaced and mumbles an apology*

Sorry… Just trying to get into the part…
Aladdin I know you…
The Slave of The Ring Do you?
Aladdin Yes — you're the genie from Uncle Abanazar's ring…
The Slave of The Ring I am The Slave of The Ring, yes. Of both rings in fact. Although never at the same time.
Aladdin That's confusing.
The Slave of The Ring Tell me about it.
Aladdin Look, I don't suppose my wish is your command is it?
The Slave of The Ring You've done this before.
Aladdin Abanazar has stolen away my lamp, my palace, my betrothed.
The Slave of The Ring Well, he's nothing if not thorough…
Aladdin I care naught for palaces of gold and magic trinkets. But seas will burn and rocks melt before I forsake Jasmine. Tell me where he has taken her.
The Slave of The Ring Africa. To his lair, deep in the Mountains of the Moon.
Aladdin Do you have magic enough to take me there?
The Slave of The Ring (*grimacing — he doesn't have a good track record*) Possibly.
Aladdin Do it, and you have my word, I will free your from your enslavement to the ring.
The Slave of The Ring (*bowing*) Truly, you are a prince amongst men.
Aladdin Will you try?
The Slave of The Ring Your wish is my command, O bravest of the brave. For you I will try extra-hard… (*Summoning up his magic*)

Act II, Scene 5

Shazzam! Abracadabra! Kalamazoo! ...And "please"...

There is a split-second Black-out and a tremendous blinding flash

The Lights come back up, Aladdin and The Slave of The Ring have gone

The CURTAINS *may now close, allowing the next scene to be set, whilst the remainder of* SCENE *5 is played out before the main tabs*

Wishee-Washee Aladdin! Ohhhhhh... Aladdin gone...
Sinbad Yep. And so's my ring. (*Ruefully*) Ah well — easy come, easy go...
Pee-Long I have to go too. The Sultana will be looking for me. (*She kisses Sinbad*)
Sinbad (*surprised*) What's that for?
Pee-Long It's the kiss I owed you.
Sinbad Thanks, but I never told you the story...
Pee-Long Erm. Well, now's not a good time. You can tell me all about it when we're married.
Sinbad Married?
Pee-Long Of course. Must run. Bye!

She flits off

Sinbad (*reflectively*) Married. (*Pause; to Wishee-Washee*) Look, I don't suppose you'd like to hear about my seven incredible voyages, would you?
Wishee-Washee (*shrugging*) If you like.
Sinbad Awesome! Well then, I could swim from the day I was conceived. My father gave me my first sailing boat when I was still in nappies, and...

They exit, Sinbad chattering animatedly, Wishee-Washee looking stupefied

The Lights fade

Scene 6

Swirling, African music. Drums. Lights up on the interior of Aladdin's palace, now transported to Darkest Africa... There are gorgeous hangings from ceiling to floor, gilt screens, and c, *a chaise-longue covered in a leopard-skin, surrounded by huge piles of opulent cushions*

Abanazar enters, dragging Princess Jasmine — now dressed in her wedding finery — behind him

Abanazar Well, my pretty. At last we are alone... Mwooohahaha!!!!

Audience participation

Princess Jasmine (*struggling attractively*) What do you want of me? Why have you brought me here?
Abanazar To be my wifelet of course! (*Leering*) The first of many... Hur hur hur hur...
Princess Jasmine But I am betrothed to Aladdin.
Abanazar Aladdin? Pooh. I hardly think your mother will approve now he's been exposed as a penniless charlatan...
Princess Jasmine I don't care. I love him.
Abanazar How romantic... Unfortunately, where royal marriages are concerned, love rarely enters into it.
Princess Jasmine I'll never marry you. Never!
Abanazar Then you will stay locked up here until you are old and lonely and wizened...
Princess Jasmine Like you, you mean.
Abanazar (*chortling*) Sticks and stones, my dear... Now, before our nuptials, my slaves have prepared a luxurious bath of warm asses' milk for you...
Princess Jasmine Asses milk?! Ugh! What kind of a sicko are you?
Abanazar I beg your pardon?
Princess Jasmine Do you seriously think I'm going to walk down the aisle reeking of horse yoghurt?
Abanazar So you will marry me?
Princess Jasmine Never!
Abanazar Now you're just being difficult...
Princess Jasmine Well take me back to where you kidnapped me from then. And take my palace back too.
Abanazar I'm warning you... Co-operate, or it will go ill with you.
Princess Jasmine You don't frighten me. I don't know the meaning of fear.

Act II, Scene 6

Abanazar Not another one — this is getting monotonous. Oh hang the formalities, let's just get down to business… Give us a kiss. (*He attempts to embrace her*)
Princess Jasmine (*fending him off*) Eeeeyuch! Never.
Abanazar Kiss me, or you die.
Princess Jasmine If I kissed you, I'd die of embarrassment.
Abanazar (*shouting*) Kiss me!
Princess Jasmine (*shouting*) Never!
Abanazar Look, it's not like I'm ugly, is it?
Princess Jasmine Durr — yes.
Abanazar Oh. (*Pause, then…*) Well kiss me anyway!

Brief Black-out. There is a sudden flash

Aladdin appears with The Slave of The Ring. He steps in front of Princess Jasmine

Aladdin Leave her alone.
Abanazar You!
Princess Jasmine Aladdin!
Aladdin Jasmine — fear not my love.

Princess Jasmine clings to Aladdin who faces down Abanzar

Abanazar (*sneering*) How touching. And where did you spring from?
Aladdin You may have stolen my lamp, but I still have magic enough.
Abanazar (*peering at The Slave of The Ring*) Hmmm. Interesting… That looks like my genie. (*He rubs his ring*)

Nothing happens. The Slave of The Ring gives him a little wave

Yup…
The Slave of The Ring Sorry — can't be in two places at once…
Abanazar Not a problem… (*He produces the lamp from within his robes and gives it a rub*)

There is another momentary Black-out, a blinding green flash

The Slave of The Lamp appears

The Slave of The Lamp Gawd 'n' Bennett! Must you keep doing that? I was just 'avin' forty winks.
Abanazar This on the other hand is *definitely* my genie.

The Slave of The Lamp Wish? Command? Bovvered?
Abanazar (*pointing to Aladdin*) Yes. I want you to make him disappear. Permanently.
The Slave of The Lamp Consider it done, me old pork sausage.
Abanazar Glad to hear it. I'll be back in five. (*Pointing to Jasmine*) And don't let her go anywhere.
Princess Jasmine Where are you going?
Abanazar To prepare the bridal bed…

Abanazar stomps off

Princess Jasmine (*turning to Aladdin*) Aladdin — do something!
Aladdin O Slave of The Ring — I command you to protect us!
The Slave of The Ring Alas, I cannot. I am a mere genie of knowledge — she is a genie of power.
The Slave of The Lamp What this tragic numpty is yappin' abaht, is that 'e is a mere low level functionary, whiles yours truly is a supreme being, innit?
The Slave of The Ring Excuse me — "tragic numpty…?" Wait a moment — that rings a bell. Hold on — I know you…
The Slave of The Lamp Do yer?
The Slave of The Ring Chantelle?
The Slave of The Lamp Reggie?
The Slave of The Ring Chantelle, is it really you?
The Slave of The Lamp Course it's me, yer great pudding…
The Slave of The Ring Good grief. I haven't seen you since genie school seven thousand years ago. You haven't changed a bit.
The Slave of The Lamp Nor ain't you, neiver (*neither*) …I used to like "like you" like — when we was at school like…
The Slave of The Ring Really? I used to like you too. Like.
The Slave of The Lamp Wicked! P'raps we oughta let our powers intermingle… (*Winking suggestively*) know what I mean?
The Slave of The Ring If only we could. But we are bound to our fates, doomed to serve these foolish mortals.
The Slave of The Lamp It's bang out of order, ain't it? Orlright, I've 'ad enough of this. You're a genie of knowledge, ain'tcha?
The Slave of The Ring Yes…
The Slave of The Lamp So where's the plan, Einstein?
The Slave of The Ring All right — I'll give you a plan… (*To Aladdin*) Tell her you'll free her if she spares you…
Aladdin What?
The Slave of The Ring Free us both from our enslavement, so we can be together for all eternity…

Act II, Scene 6

Aladdin But then I won't have any more wishes…
The Slave of The Ring No. You will have the most precious gift of all, Aladdin — your life. Not to mention the girl of your dreams by your side.
Aladdin (*considering*) True. But in order to free the slave from the lamp, I need to be master of the lamp… How do we get the lamp from Abanazar?
Princess Jasmine Leave that to me…
Abanazar (*off*) Fi Fie Fo Fum… I can smell Aladdin's bum! Ha ha ha ha ha!
Princess Jasmine He's coming.
Aladdin (*to The Slave of The Ring*) Deal?
The Slave of The Ring Deal.
Aladdin (*to The Slave of The Lamp*) Deal?

Pause

The Slave of The Lamp Oh, go on then…
Aladdin Cool. (*To Princess Jasmine*) What are you going to do?
Princess Jasmine Wait and see…
Abanazar (*off*) Here I come, ready or not…
Aladdin Whatever it is, it had better be good…
Princess Jasmine Watch and learn, laundry boy. When the going gets tough, the posh get going…

Abanazar enters

Abanazar (*doing a double-take upon seeing Aladdin*) What's he still doing here?! (*To The Slave of The Lamp*) Didn't I tell you to destroy him utterly?
The Slave of The Lamp Nah — you said to make him disappear.
Abanazar So why's he still here?
The Slave of The Lamp Well gimme a chance. I'm getting around to it…
Abanazar Well get around to it a bit quicker — destroy him!
The Slave of The Lamp Are you giving me an order, laughing-boy?
Abanazar Of course it's a ruddy order ——
Princess Jasmine (*interrupting him*) Wait! …O Abanazar, my illustrious Lord and Master…
Abanazar Eh?

Princess Jasmine — very slinky all of a sudden — slides across to where Abanazar is standing, and trails one seductive finger around his shoulder

Princess Jasmine I have a proposition for you...
Abanazar (*narrowly*) Go on...
Princess Jasmine Spare Aladdin and I will marry you...
Aladdin Jasmine, no!
Abanazar (*incredulous*) Marry me?
Princess Jasmine (*hissing to Aladdin*) It's the only way.
Abanazar What, marry me properly?
Princess Jasmine Yes.
Abanazar What... with kissing and everything?
Princess Jasmine Everything.
Abanazar You'll iron my dishdash?
Princess Jasmine Yes.
Abanazar And cook my favourite dinner?
Jasmine What is it?
Abanazar Curried locusts.
Princess Jasmine Ugh... Yes.
Abanazar And do the washing-up?
Princess Jasmine Everything.
Abanazar (*rubbing his hands in unholy glee*) All right — now you're talking!
Princess Jasmine Do we have a deal?
Abanazar Do we?! I should cocoa...
Princess Jasmine Excellent. In that case, we must have a drink to celebrate...
Abanazar Too right. (*To the Slave of the Lamp*) Slave — the finest sherbet...
Princess Jasmine Sherbet? (*Pouting*) I was thinking of something a little stronger...
Abanazar Stronger?
Princess Jasmine (*sultry*) To help me get in the mood...
Abanazar Oh — right, er.. yes, OK then. Slave — a jug of ginger beer. (*Recklessly*) On the rocks.
Princess Jasmine I was thinking more of... champagne...
Abanazar Champagne?
Princess Jasmine (*wide-eyed insouciance*) You do like champagne, don't you, my love?
Abanazar Well, I er...
Princess Jasmine I mean, a sophisticated man of the world like yourself... Of course you do. How silly of me...
Abanazar Yes... Silly... (*To The Slave of The Lamp*) Er... Slave!
The Slave of The Lamp Wassup?
Abanazar The Bollinger 'sixty-three I think...
The Slave of The Lamp One bottle or two?

Act II, Scene 6   73

Princess Jasmine sighs, leans on Abanazar and artlessly slips one shoulder out of her top

Princess Jasmine (*fanning herself with her free hand*) Oh it's getting so hot in here...

Abanazar gazes lasciviously at the glimpse of Princess Jasmine's shapely shoulder

Abanazar (*thickly*) Better make it a crate...
Aladdin (*hissing*) Jasmine!
The Slave of The Ring (*aside*) Stay cool, Romeo...
The Slave of The Lamp As you command, O Fancy Pants...

Split second Black-out. There is small flash — The Slave of The Lamp produces a crate of champagne, lifts out a bottle, pops a cork, and pours two glasses

Abanazar (*sipping tentatively*) Oh. It's full of bubbles...
Princess Jasmine (*coquettishly*) They're all part of the fun...
Abanazar I say, d'you know, it's not half bad... (*He slurps it down greedily*)
Princess Jasmine Course it's not. Here — have another... (*She passes him her full glass and proceeds to refill his empty one*)
Abanazar Don't mind if I do... Not too strong is it?
Princess Jasmine Strong? Hardly. It's just a fizzy drink — like lemonade really...
Abanazar (*already feeling the effects*) That'sh all right then... Aladdin, my boy — have one, why don't you? (*He downs his second glass*)

Again Princess Jasmine presents him with another full one

Aladdin Thanks...
Abanazar No hard feelings?
Aladdin No hard feelings.
Abanazar Sure? ...About me shutting you in the cave, I mean.
Aladdin Course not.
Abanazar And leaving you to rot.
Aladdin As if...
Abanazar And stealing the lamp.
Aladdin Well, it should have been yours in the first place really, shouldn't it?
Abanazar Ha! I'll drink to that...
Aladdin Cheers.

Abanazar Mud in your eye… (*Finishing his third glass and becoming more visibly tiddly*) And… I mean, you're not sore about me getting the girl in the end?
Aladdin Now how could I be angry with my own uncle?
Abanazar Uncle… Ha ha! That'sh a good one… Uncle… Hahahaha… (*Aside*) God, what a loser…

Princess Jasmine passes him another glass of champagne which he guzzles

(*Staggering, managing to right himself, peering blearily at Aladdin*) Oooopsh. Hey — wassssup? You're not drinking, you lightweight!
Aladdin Erm, well I don't have anything to drink out of…
Abanazar Nothing to drink out of??? We can't have that! That is nuffink less than out-hic-rageous… (*Casting around drunkenly; hauling the lamp out of his robes and handing it over*) Here, use thish.
Aladdin Thanks very much.
Abanazar Pleasure. Down the hatch.
Aladdin Bottoms up… (*Miming taking a sip and peering at Abanazar with interest as the magician drains his fourth glass of champagne*) Are you all right?
Abanazar Courshe I'm all right… I'm not as drunk as thinkle peep I am… Hic.
Aladdin Oh good…
Abanazar (*now very lairy*) More shampoo!

The Slave of the Lamp pops another bottle and tops him up… Abanazar guzzles. Princess Jasmine mimes sipping from her glass

Come on, Aladdin, you pussycat! Get some down yer… Tee hee hee… (*Slurring badly now*) Ladiesh and gennelmenn… a boast… I mean… a roasht… hic…
Princess Jasmine A toast.
Abanazar Thassit… A toasht. (*Climbing unsteadily on to the chaise-lounge*) To my favourite thingsh in all the worl'… To Gold. To Girlsh. And to Glory.
Aladdin Gold, girls, and glory!
Abanazar (*draining his glass*) Bloody lovely… Hic. (*He falls over backwards into the large pile of cushions and soft furnishings and passes out*)

The Slave of The Ring crosses to peer down at him

The Slave of The Ring Absolutely paralytic.

Act II, Scene 6

Aladdin (*exhibiting a little Abanazar-style unholy glee*) And the lamp is mine! Mine!
Princess Jasmine Ours.
Aladdin (*catching himself*) Er... That's what I meant... (*Turning to her seriously*) Jasmine — that was a good plan.
Princess Jasmine (*modestly*) Thank you, Aladdin.
Aladdin Clever as well as beautiful... I can see I shall have to watch my step with you.
Princess Jasmine Better believe it, Bucko.

They laugh and embrace

The Slave of The Lamp Ahem. Ain't you forgettin somefink a bit crooshal?
The Slave of The Ring Release us. Fulfill your vow.
Aladdin I will. I promise. But first, just a few more little wishes — if you don't mind?

The Slaves of The Lamp and The Ring exchange glances... Then nod

The Slave of The Ring Seven thousand years cooped up in there. What's a couple more hours?
Aladdin Cool. In that case, fly me to China!
The Slave of The Lamp Your wish is our command. Innit.

Song 9 (Aladdin, Princess Jasmine, The Slave of The Lamp and The Slave of The Ring)

This too can be brought on to the forestage, to allow the main tabs to close behind them and the scene to be set for the grand finale

At the end of the song they can either simply dance off or — if it can be managed with all four of them — exit to another flash

Meanwhile, Abanazar wakes up and makes his way to the front — through the main tabs if necessary...

Abanazar Oh my head... What happened? Ah yes, I remember... Gold! Girls! Glory! I've got the lot. And the lamp... I've got the lamp... Hahahaha... The lamp? (*Shouting*) Slave! (*No response*) Slave? Where is it? Where's it gone Precious? No — I've been tricked. I've been diddled. Curse you Aladdin! Curse you! Aaaaaaaaaaaaaaaaaaaaaaaargggghhh!!!! (*Raging, he runs madly around the forestage, tearing at his clothes*)

The Lights fade

Scene 7

Pomp and Circumstance music Chinese style once again. Lights up on the glittering throne room of Ming the Mirthless. Grand ceremonial entrance of the assembled court

Once again, the Grand Vizier strikes his staff of office three times on the floor

Herald All kow-tow before his Imperial Highness, Ming the Mirthless, Sultan of Ching-Chong, Ping-Pong, and Oooooagadoogoo…

The Herald bows and exits

Chip-Chop-Ow steps forward and swings his donger to connect with the giant gong. This time he gets the sound effect of a huge reverberating dong. His customary inscrutability briefly cracks as he does an uncharacteristic little Tim Henman-style fist pump. As one, the court kow-tows

The Sultan and Sultana enter and sit upon the twin thrones

Chip-Chop-Ow takes up his place behind No-Lo-Fat, exchanging his donger for his chopper

Widow Twankee is pushed on to stand to one side

The Grand Vizier Stunned silence for his Most Imperial Highness, Ming the Mirthless, Sultan of Ching-Chong, Ping——
Ming the Mirthless (*interrupting him*) Oh do shut up.
No-Lo-Fat (*briskly*) Yes, straight to business. Item number one, if you please…
The Grand Vizier Item number one: Summary head-chop of Widow Twankee on charges of aiding and abetting the wilful deceit of the royal court in the matter of Aladdin and his…
Ming the Mirthless (*interrupting*) Oh, for heaven's sake stop it.
No-Lo-Fat Stop what?
Ming the Mirthless All this. All these head-chops.
No-Lo-Fat Why?
Ming the Mirthless Because chopping the wretched woman's head off isn't going to bring Jasmine back, is it?
No-Lo-Fat That's not the point. It's all because of her horrid little sprog of a son that we're in this mess.

Act II, Scene 7

Widow Twankee (*bridling*) 'Ere! Don't you talk about my Aladdin like that…
No-Lo-Fat (*stomping down from her throne to confront Widow Twankee*) I shall talk about him however I like! I am the Sultana.
Widow Twankee Oh no you won't!
No-Lo-Fat Oh yes I will!

They are nose to nose now

Ming the Mirthless (*separating them*) Oh be quiet, both of you… I just want my little Jasmine back.
Widow Twankee And I just want my Aladdin back.

Glaring, No-Lo-Fat returns to her throne

Ming the Mirthless Yes, I know you do. Both our children are missing. Come here — sit with us.
Widow Twankee Well that's very civil of you, squire. (*Perching on the arm of No-Lo-Fat's throne*) Budge up.
No-Lo-Fat Well! Never in all my life have I been so insulted…
Widow Twankee Well you want to get out more then.
No-Lo-Fat I am not putting up with this, I —

The Herald runs on

Herald Majesties! The Golden Palace of Sum-Tin-Wong materialised outside the East Gate to the City, not ten minutes since!

Uproar! Another messenger enters and whispers to the Grand Vizier

The Grand Vizier (*announcing*) Their Imperial Highnesses, Prince Aladdin and Princess Jasmine.

Aladdin and Princess Jasmine sweep on, followed by Sinbad, Pee-Long, Wishee-Washee and Noo-Noo

Ming the Mirthless Jasmine!
Princess Jasmine Daddy!
Widow Twankee Aladdin!
Aladdin Mother!
Princess Jasmine Mother!
Ming the Mirthless Aladdin!
Aladdin Daddy!

No-Lo-Fat Jasmine! (*Pause*) Hold on a minute… Prince Aladdin?
Princess Jasmine (*flashing a ring with an enormous diamond*) We got married — isn't it wonderful?
No-Lo-Fat No — it's a disgrace!
Widow Twankee Too right it is — I didn't get to ride an elephant.
Ming the Mirthless Well I'm very happy for you, dear — and for you, my boy. Very well done. (*Aside to Aladdin*) I'm glad she's your responsibility now.
No-Lo-Fat What on earth are you saying, O Husband?! Have you lost your mind? This miscreant deceived us, was responsible for our only daughter being kidnapped and spirited halfway round the world, and now he's gone and married her without so much as a "by your leave" ——
Ming the Mirthless (*interrupting her*) Oh for goodness sake, give it a rest woman.
No-Lo-Fat (*astounded*) I beg your pardon!
Ming the Mirthless Nag, nag, nag. It's no wonder they call me Ming the ruddy Mirthless with you going on at me all the time. Why don't you just put a sock in it for once!
No-Lo-Fat Ooooh, how very dare you!
Ming the Mirthless How dare I? How dare I? I dare because I'm the ruddy Sultan, capiche?
Princess Jasmine Go on Daddy, you tell her.
No-Lo-Fat Jasmine!
Ming the Mirthless I've had just about enough of being told what to do by you. By everybody. In fact, I've had just about enough of being Sultan. It's a miserable job. Aladdin, my boy — I abdicate. You're married to my daughter, you've got twice the common sense of anyone I've ever met, and you're not afraid of anything. I can't think of better qualifications to be Sultan. So there you are — keys to the kingdom. All yours. (*He hands over a set of outsize keys from around his neck*)
Aladdin Wow. Thanks.
No-Lo-Fat (*gobsmacked*) But what are we going to do?
Ming the Mirthless We are going to retire to a minor palace in the country, where I am going to grow dahlias and build model aeroplanes, and you are going to become a modest, gracious and compliant wife. Or I shall take a harem of lewd Scandanavian strumpets, and you won't get a look in! Well?
No-Lo-Fat (*swallowing hard*) Very well dear, as you say…
Ming the Mirthless That's more like it. Right, Aladdin — over to you.
Aladdin Your Highness, I'm honoured.
Ming the Mirthless Don't be. Trust me, it's a pain in the bum.

Act II, Scene 7

Ming the Mirthless and No-Lo-Fat retire to one side. Music as Aladdin and Princess Jasmine ascend to the thrones. The Grand Vizier steps forward

The Grand Vizier (*intoning*) O Lord Aladdin, Sultan of Ching-Chong, Ping-Pong, and Oooooagadoogoo. What is your first command?
Aladdin Bring on the prisoners!

Mrs Cheng and Abanazar are unceremoniously bundled on by Hoo-Poo and Hee-Pong

Audience participation

Behold! The Great Abanazar and Mrs Cheng — Queen of the Yangtse Pirates. As raddled and poisonous a pair of pantomime villains as you could never wish to meet on a dark night. (*He stands and comes down towards them*) These two sought to do down my family, my friends, and myself. They failed. What shall we do with them?
All Head Chop!
Aladdin That would be too easy. A Sultan must exercise wisdom, and temper justice with mercy.
Ming the Mirthless (*aside to Widow Twankee*) God, he's good.
Princess Jasmine What have you got to say for yourselves?
Abanazar Aladdin, my dear boy… There's obviously been a misunderstanding…
Mrs Cheng Indeed — as you can see, I am just a demure lady traveller…
Abanazar And I am your kindly uncle…
Mrs Cheng An unfortunate case of mistaken identity…
Abanazar We'll see ourselves out…

They turn to go but find their way blocked by Hoo-Poo and Hee Pong

Aladdin Then these two rings do not rightly belong to you?
Abanazar Yes! Yes! They do.
Mrs Cheng Give them back!
Abanazar We wants them, Precious!
Aladdin Have them. (*He tosses the rings*)

They catch them and both rub feverishly at them. Nothing happens

Unfortunately, you will find them of no use. I have freed The Slave of The Ring.
Abanazar You what?

Mrs Cheng You fool.
Abanazar You idiot.
Aladdin And here he is.

The Slave of The Ring saunters on

Abanazar You'll be telling me next you've released The Slave of The Lamp too…
Aladdin I have. And here she is…

The Slave of The Lamp comes on to join The Slave of The Ring

Abanazar You must be stark raving mad, boy. You've given away a lifetime's power — untold riches beyond imagining.
Aladdin What need, when I have everything a man could wish for?
Ming the Mirthless The keys to a kingdom.
Princess Jasmine The love of his life.
Sinbad And respect and fame through all the lands of the Orient.
Abanazar Gold, girls and glory! Gah — it's so unfair!
Mrs Cheng (*to Aladdin*) Look, how's about I get this old humbug Shanghaied aboard a slow boat to Sumatra for you? In exchange for a reduced sentence?
Aladdin You two really do deserve each other. (*To The Slave of The Lamp*) Send them to The Cave of a Thousand Rubies.
Abanazar
Mrs Cheng } (*together*) Nooooooooooooooooooooooooooo!!!
The Slave of The Lamp Your wish is my pleasure. (*She clicks her fingers*)

Brief Black-out. Flash bang

Abanazar and Mrs Cheng vanish

Princess Jasmine (*admiringly*) Oh Aladdin. You can be very implacable.
Aladdin Not really, I've already had the place stocked up with dogfood and Irn Bru. They'll have enough to survive on for seven years, then we'll let them out.
Sinbad If they haven't killed each other by then.
Widow Twankee One lives in hope…
Pee-Long They can count all their treasure over and over…
Sinbad But they won't be able to enjoy one penny of it.
Princess Jasmine Cruel but fair.
Aladdin (*turning to the genies*) O Slave of The Lamp. I hold true to my vow and release you from your servitude. Go in freedom.

Act II, Scene 7

Princess Jasmine And with all our love.
The Slave of The Ring Thank you, Aladdin.

The two genies take hands

Ready dear?
The Slave of The Lamp Too blinkin' right.
The Slave of The Ring Shazzam!
The Slave of The Lamp Yeah — see ya.

Flash. The Slaves of The Ring and The Lamp disappear for good

Aladdin turns to Hoo-Poo and Hee-Pong

Aladdin And as for you two...
Hoo-Poo What, us?
Aladdin Yes you. It seems that every time you had the chance to do the right thing, you did the opposite.
Hee-Pong Ah.
Aladdin Not really what's required in the police force, is it?
Hoo-Poo (*aside*) Obviously, he hasn't met many policemen either...
Aladdin Hoo-Poo, Hee-Pong — you're fired.

Hoo-Poo and Hee-Pong collapse in a blubbering heap on the floor, embracing each other

Hoo-Poo Fired? ...But what we gonna do?
Hee-Pong Well, there's a vacancy for Queen of the Yangtse Pirates.
Hoo-Poo There is?

Suddenly, the sound effect of a large ship's foghorn is heard. Hoo-Poo and Hee-Pong stare at each other

Hey — that's an oil tanker off the coast of Somalia... (*or insert other topical pirate hotspot*)
Hee-Pong Wicked! You fetch speedboat, I get rocket-launcher!

They rush off, each trying to hold the other back

Aladdin (*turning to Sinbad*) Sinbad, my good friend, for all your kindnesses, I am forever in your debt. Will you stay in Peking and become my first minister?
Sinbad Thank you, my friend, but fresh voyages await, new adventures and tall tales to be written.

Pee-Long Anyway, you can't have two principal boys in one pantomime — that would just be silly…

Sinbad Besides, I want to show my bride the wonders of Arabia.

Widow Twankee (*aside to Pee-Long*) Sand.

Wishee-Washee Yeah, and Wishee-Washee going along too. Time to splead wings. See world. Make whoopee. Can't stay laundry boy f'rever…

Aladdin No indeed.

Widow Twankee 'Ere, hang on a minute. Everyone seems to be getting an 'appy ending — what about me?

Aladdin Well what would you like?

Widow Twankee Well with you running the country, and Wishee-Washee off to see the world, I could do with a bit of help around the laundry…

Princess Jasmine Don't be silly. You don't need to run the laundry any more — you can come and live with us. Or we'll build you a nice little summer palace all of your own.

Widow Twankee Well, that's very nice of you dear, but I wouldn't know where to put meself. (*Holding up her large hands*) See these? These hands were meant to go in buckets — that's where they belong. Not in a palace.

Princess Jasmine Well, if you're sure…

Widow Twankee Oh I'm sure. But what I could really do with is a man about the place. To do the heavy lifting… (*Hoiking up her enormous padded bosom*)

Aladdin Take your pick.

Widow Twankee Coo, ta very much. (*Looking at Chip-Chop-Ow's inscrutable countenance*) This one looks strong as an ox, but I don't know if I could get used to that great big chopper of his… (*Clapping the Grand Vizier on the shoulder*) Actually, I think I'll take this one.

The Grand Vizier (*horrified*) Me? No! I am refined higher official of Imperial Civil Service.

Widow Twankee Well, now you're my assistant slopper-out. But if you're very good, I might find some extra-mural duties for you too… (*Winking*) Know what I mean?

The Grand Vizier Noooooo…

Aladdin Well, that's settled then. Does that count as a happy ending?

The Grand Vizier No it doesn't.

All Oh yes it does! Hurray!

Song 10 (Aladdin and Princess Jasmine, Sinbad and Pee-Long,
Widow Twankee and the Grand Vizier,
Ming the Mirthless and No-Lo-Fat, and Wishee-Washee)

Act II, Scene 7   83

Any remaining courtiers and attendants backing them if required

Curtain

Walkdown and Curtain *call order:*

Yangtse pirates
Attendants, courtiers, Herald, Grand Vizier, Chip-Chop-Ow
Wishee-Washee and Noo-Noo
Slaves of The Ring and The Lamp
Hoo-Poo and Hee-Pong
Ming the Mirthless and No-Lo-Fat
Abanazar and Mrs Cheng
Sinbad and Pee-Long
Aladdin and Princess Jasmine
Widow Twankee

After the bows have been taken, the final rhyme is delivered…

Widow Twankee So ends the final chapter in our oriental story.
The Slave of The Ring A tale of magic lamps and rings —
Aladdin And girls and gold and glory!
Princess Jasmine And of true love and high romance — sweet dreams that we fulfill…
Widow Twankee 'Ere! Pass the sickbag, Wishee-Washee — she's making me feel ill!
Sinbad I've found the very best of friends amongst the Pekingese…
Pee-Long Now we're off to find adventure upon the shining seas!
Wishee-Washee Yah!
Abanazar My wicked plans have come to naught — it's more than I can bear.
Mrs Cheng Now I'm stuck with him for seven years — that really is unfair.
Hoo-Poo We had to leave the police force to pursue a new career…
Hee-Pong I've retrained as a pirate…
Hoo-Poo And I'm a buccaneer.
Hoo-Poo
Hee-Pong } (*together*) Har-harr!
Ming the Mirthless It's time for me to settle down and lead a quieter life…
No-Lo-Fat I'm going to pretend to be an obedient little wife.
Widow Twankee That's enough moralising for another year, I need to get me make-up off — I'm gasping for a beer.

The Slave of The Lamp Innit…
Ming the Mirthless We hope that you enjoyed the show. What a jolly time we've had!
Widow Twankee With this tale of Widow Twankee…
Aladdin Of Aladdin…
Sinbad And Sinbad!
Widow Twankee So good night and…
All Merry Christmas! (*Or Happy New Year*)

Song 11 (Final number – the company)

Final bow

CURTAIN

FURNITURE AND PROPERTY LIST

ACT I
Scene 1

On stage: Overhead sign reads "Old Peking" in oriental lettering
Pagodas to either side
Strings of colourful Chinese lanterns

Off stage: Bundle wrapped in spotted handkerchief (**Sinbad**)
Tricycle (**Wishee-Washee**)
Custard pie (**Widow Twankee**)
Besom broom and megaphone (**Hoo-poo**)
Bone-shaker bicycle. *On it*: basket. *In it*: Pekingese glove puppet, Blue flag (**Hee-Pong**)

Scene 2

Set: Tent
Hanging fabric
Animal skins
Big pots

Strike: Sign "Old Peking"
Pagodas
Strings of lanterns

Personal: Ring (**Abanazar**)

Scene 3

Set: Sign "Happy Tub Chinese Laundry"
Two washing lines cross the width of the stage. *On it*: string of sheets, knickerbockers, other comic laundry items, large sheet, teeny flannel, large fluffy bath towel
Giant wash tub

Strike: Tent
Hanging fabric
Animal skins
Big pots

Off stage: Foam rubber truncheons (**Hoo-Poo and Hee-Pong**)
Chopper, Tiny pair of nail scissors (**Executioner**)
Ice cream scoop (**Chip-Chop-Ow**)

Scene 4

Off stage: Scooters (**Hoo-Poo and Hee-Pong**)
Foam rubber mallet and poster (**Hoo-Poo**)
Coolie hat (**Aladdin**)
Handbag. *In it*: turban (**Widow Twankee**)
Purse of money (**Abanazar**)

Scene 5

Strike: Sign "Happy Tub Chinese Laundry"
Two washing lines cross the width of the stage
Giant wash tub

Scene 6

Set: Chairs, Table. *On it*: tea-set, sugar
One washing line. *On it*: some washing

Off stage: Tape measure (**Chip-Chop-Ow**)

Scene 7

Set: Poster on the proscenium arch

Strike: Table and chairs
A washing line

Off stage: Turban, coolie hat (**Sinbad**)
Foam rubber nunchuks, cuffs (**Hoo-Poo and Hee-Ping**)

Scene 8

Set: Outside the cave

Strike: Poster on the proscenium arch

Off stage: Coil of stout rope (**Aladdin**)

Personal: Ring (**Abanazar**)

Furniture and Property List

Scene 9

Set: Inside the cave. *Around it*: piles of gold, jewels and lamp

Strike: Outside the cave scene

ACT II
Scene 1

On stage: Twin thrones
Hanging gong
Red and gold banners
Oriental motifs

Off Stage: Tray of savouries, mahogany chest. *In it*: piles of gold coin and jewels, box (**Attendant**)
Card (**Messenger**)
Donger, Chopper (**Chip-Chop-Ow**)

Scene 2

Strike: Twin thrones
Hanging gong
Red and gold banners
Oriental motifs

Off stage: Knives and pistols (**Pirates**)
Foam rubber cudgel (**Wong-Ki-I**)

Scene 3

Set: Table and chairs
Kitchen table. *On it*: lamp
One washing line. On it: different array of comical laundry items

Off stage: Basket (**Wishee-Washee**)
Folded slip of paper (**Messenger**)
Array of lamps (**Abanazar**)

Scene 4

Strike: Table and chairs
Kitchen table
Washing line

Off stage:	Huge bag of sweets (**Widow Twankee**)

Scene 5

Off stage:	Small pouch. *In it*: ring (**Sinbad**)

Scene 6

Set:	Gorgeous hangings Gilt screens Chaise-longue. *Covering it*: leopard skin. *Surrounding it*: piles of cushions
Off stage:	Crate of champagne, glasses (**The Slave of The Lamp**) Lamp (**Abanazar**)

Scene 7

Set:	Throne room
Strike:	Gorgeous hangings Gilt screens Chaise-lounge
Off stage:	Diamond ring (**Princess Jasmine**) Set of outsize keys (**Ming the Mirthless**) Rings (**Aladdin**)

LIGHTING PLOT

Practical fitting required: nil
Various interior and exterior settings

ACT I, SCENE 1

To open: General lighting

Cue 1	**Hoo-Poo** and **Hee-Pong** run hell for leather in the opposite direction *Lights fade*	(Page 11)

ACT I, SCENE 2

To open: General lighting

Cue 2	**Abanazar** rubs his hands together and chuckles horribly *Brief Black-out then a blinding flash*	(Page 11)
Cue 3	**Abanazar** clicks his fingers *Flash. After a few moments Lights come up*	(Page 13)
Cue 4	**The Slave of The Ring** sidles off *Lights fade*	(Page 13)

ACT I, SCENE 3

To open: General lighting

Cue 5	**Princess Jasmine**: "Where are you now...?" *Lights fade*	(Page 20)

ACT I, SCENE 4

To open: General lighting

Cue 6	**Aladdin** and **Abanazar** go off *Lights fade*	(Page 25)

ACT I, SCENE 5

To open: Greeny-blue lights, silver shimmers across the bare stage

Cue 7	**Mrs Cheng**: "I am a pantomime villain! Mwoah — hahahahaha!!!!" *Lights change and lightning splits*	(Page 26)
Cue 8	**Crew**: "Mwoah-hahahaha!!!" *Lights back to normal; greeny-blue lights*	(Page 27)
Cue 9	After the song, **the pirates** disperse through the audience *Lights fade*	(Page 27)

ACT I, SCENE 6

To open: General lighting

Cue 10	**Wishee-Washee** sits on the floor and starts bawling like a baby *Lights fade*	(Page 33)

ACT I, SCENE 7

To open: General lighting

Cue 11	**Pee-Long**: "...neither of us will have him." Then scuttles off *Lights fade*	(Page 34)

ACT I, SCENE 8

To open: General lighting

Cue 12	**Abanazar** rubs his magic ring *Brief Black-out and a flash*	(Page 35)

ACT I, SCENE 9

To open: Narrow shaft of daylight overhead. Apart from that pitch black

Cue 13	**Aladdin**: "It's awfully dark..." *Flickering ghostly lights*	(Page 37)
Cue 14	**Aladdin**: "Now let me see... WOW!" *Low spotlight*	(Page 37)

Lighting Plot

Cue 15	**Aladdin**: "Uncle?" *Shaft of light goes out. Dark*	(Page 39)
Cue 16	**Aladdin** rubs the lamps *Green flash*	(Page 39)
Cue 17	**The Slave of The Lamp**: "Let us depart instanter!" *Flash and Black-out*	(Page 40)

ACT II, SCENE 1

To open: General lighting

Cue 18	**No-Lo-Fat**: "...your head will be forfeit!" *Lights fade*	(Page 48)

ACT II, SCENE 2

To open: Greeny-blue lights

Cue 19	**Hoo-Poo** and **Hee-Pong** are engulfed and bundled offstage by the pirates *Lights fade*	(Page 53)

ACT II, SCENE 3

To open: General lighting

Cue 20	**Abanazar**: "Hocus-Pocus, Sim-Sala-Bim, Alakazam!" *Brief Black-out then a green flash*	(Page 57)
Cue 21	**The Slave of The Lamp**: "Your wish is my command I s'pose..." *Brief Black-out then a flash*	(Page 57)
Cue 22	**Wishee-Washee**: "Break bad news..." then trots off *Lights fade*	(Page 58)

ACT II, SCENE 4

To open: General lighting

Cue 23	**Widow Twankee** and **Wishee-Washee** go off in the wrong direction *Lights fade*	(Page 62)

ACT II, SCENE 5

To open: Lighting changes

Cue 24	**Wishee-Washee**: "Aladdin — no!" **Aladdin** rubs the ring *Split-second Black-out and mighty flash*	(Page 65)
Cue 25	**The Slave of The Ring**: "Abracadabra! Kalamazoo! ... And "please"..." *Split-second Black-out and a blinding flash, then lights come back up*	(Page 67)
Cue 26	**Sinbad** and **Wishee-Washee** exit *Lights fade*	(Page 67)

ACT II, SCENE 6

To open: General lighting

Cue 27	**Abanazar**: "Well kiss me anyway!" *Brief Black-out then flash*	(Page 69)
Cue 28	**Abanazar** produces the lamp and gives it a rub *Brief Black-out then a blinding green flash*	(Page 69)
Cue 29	**The Slave of The Lamp**: "As you command, O Fancy Pants..." *Split second Black-out, then a small flash*	(Page 73)
Cue 30	**Abanazar**: "Aaaarggh!" Then he runs around the forestage, tearing at his clothes *Lights fade*	(Page 75)

ACT II, SCENE 7

To open: General lighting

Cue 31	**The Slave of The Lamp**: "Your wish is my pleasure." Then she clicks her fingers *Brief Black-out then a flash*	(Page 80)
Cue 32	The Slave of The Lamp: "Yeah — see ya." *Flash*	(Page 81)

EFFECTS PLOT

ACT I

Cue 1	After a few moments when the entire cast enter *Music**	(Page 1)
Cue 2	**Widow Twankee**: "...to be the spectacular opening number..." *Music fizzles out*	(Page 1)
Cue 3	**Hee-Pong**: "Hoo-Poo!" *Loud dong*	(Page 8)
Cue 4	Beginning of SCENE 2 *Mystical Eastern music*	(Page 11)
Cue 5	**Abanazar** enters *Music fades*	(Page 11)
Cue 6	**Abanazar** rubs his hands together *Loud bang*	(Page 11)
Cue 7	**The Slave of The Ring**: "Shazzam! Abracadabra! And Kalamazoo!) *Puff of smoke*	(Page 13)
Cue 8	Beginning of SCENE 3 *Happy Chinese music*	(Page 13)
Cue 9	**Aladdin** enters *Music fades*	(Page 13)
Cue 10	**No-Lo-Fat**: "Quite so. Chip-Chop-Ow!" *Sinister chords*	(Page 18)
Cue 11	**Hoo-Poo** and **Hee-Pong** park their scooters and ascend the stage *Sound effect of hammering*	(Page 21)

* *The music cues may be played by musicians if present*

Cue 12	Lights up on SCENE 5 *Mysterious oriental music*	(Page 25)
Cue 13	Shadowy figures flit across the stage *Music changes to the loud bit*	(Page 25)
Cue 14	**The pirates** race about the stage *Sinister gong sounds*	(Page 25)
Cue 15	**Mrs Cheng**: "I am a pantomime villain! Mwoah — hahahahaha!!!" *Thunder crashes and Captain Nemo organ music is heard*	(Page 26)
Cue 16	After Song 5 *Jolly Chinese music*	(Page 27)
Cue 17	**Widow Twankee**: "Just a little misunderstanding that's all..." *Hammering on the door*	(Page 30)
Cue 18	**Abanazar**: "Oh all right. Open — please?" *Creaking, graunching rumble*	(Page 36)
Cue 19	**Abanazar**: "You have less time than you think" *Music*	(Page 37)
Cue 20	**Aladdin**: "It's awfully dark." *Screaming voices*	(Page 37)
Cue 21	**Aladdin**: "Shriek all you like — you can't hurt me." *Voices and noises abate then small sounds of disappointment*	(Page 37)
Cue 22	**Aladdin**: "Uncle!!!" *Graunching noise*	(Page 39)
Cue 23	**The Slave of The Lamp**: "Touchy.." *Music*	(Page 41)

ACT II

Cue 24	Beginning of SCENE 1 *Music*	(Page 42)
Cue 25	**Chip-Chop-Ow** swings a donger to connect with the giant gong *Sound effect of a three inch dinner gong*	(Page 42)

Effects Plot

Cue 26	Child attendant slugs the gong *Sound effect of a huge reverberating dong*	(Page 42)
Cue 27	Small attendant thrusts the donger back to **Chip-Chop-Ow** and saunters off *Music*	(Page 42)
Cue 28	Lights up on SCENE 2 *Gong sounds*	(Page 48)
Cue 29	**Abanazar**: "New lamps for old!" *Hammering on the door*	(Page 55)
Cue 30	**Wishee-Washee**: "Yeah, you probably light. Here.." *Music*	(Page 56)
Cue 31	**Abanazar**: "Oh I'm sure..." and **Wishee-Washee** is about to hand over the lamp *Music*	(Page 56)
Cue 32	**Aladdin**: "No chance." *Music*	(Page 64)
Cue 33	**Wishee-Washee**: "Aladdin — no!" and **Aladdin** rubs the ring *Mighty bang*	(Page 65)
Cue 34	At the beginning of SCENE 6 *African music*	(Page 68)
Cue 35	At the beginning of SCENE 7 *Pomp and circumstance Chinese style music*	(Page 76)
Cue 36	**Chip-Chop-Ow** swings his donger to connect with the giant gong *Sound effect of a huge reverberating dong*	(Page 76)
Cue 37	**Hoo-Poo**: "There is?" *Sound effect of a large ship's foghorn*	(Page 82)